Praise for *Why I Love Homeschooling*

"The great thing about this book is that it gives you an idea of how home-schooling has worked in 24 different families, not just one. If you are considering homeschooling, your ways will be different, but at least you won't go into it thinking there's only one right way. The great thing about homeschooling, which differentiates it from traditional public or private schooling, is that it can accommodate the wonderful ways that all of us human beings differ from one another. The real leaders in any successful homeschooling program are the children. The parents learn to follow them. That message, in one way or another, runs through every one of the essays in this book."
— Peter Gray, Research Professor at Boston College and author of *Free to Learn*

"As interest in homeschooling soars, this collection of honest, heartfelt essays provides encouragement and inspiration for new homeschooling families—as well as those of us who have been on this educational path for a long time."
— Kerry McDonald, author of *Unschooled: Raising Curious, Well-Educated Children Outside the Conventional Classroom*

"Whether you come to homeschool by choice, by accident, or under duress, the combined voices of the families who share their experiences in this volume will be a source of comfort and inspiration to you! Homeschooling may be a bold choice, but it is also a natural one—and well worth the challenges. Welcome to this joyful journey! And rest assured that there are many on this path with you who are ready and willing to lend support."
— Rachel DeMille, TJEd.org, "An Education to Match Your Mission"

"The best decision I ever made was to homeschool my children. But it was a scary decision to make, and I read lots of information before I made the leap. Brynn and Kathy have gathered so many homeschoolers in one place to create a great resource for parents considering homeschooling. This is the book you can rely on to create a realistic picture of homeschooling for you and your family. What I needed in order to start homeschooling was an extra dose of bravery, and I got it from talking to parents like the ones in this book. So pick up this book for the last bit of bravery you need to make homeschooling the solution for your family."
— Penelope Trunk, blogger, life coach, and author of *The Power of Mentors* and *The New American Dream*

"Somewhere along the way, society began to believe that government in-stitutions could better meet the individual needs of each child than parents

could. Preposterous! Parents are the experts on their children, and it is parents who can best customize their children's education to meet their unique needs. This book tells the stories of parents who have broken from the status quo to provide their kids with the best possible chance at a great education. It is a refreshing read for parents who know there must be a better way!"
— **Connor Boyack, author of *Passion-Driven Education***

"If you have ever wondered whether to homeschool your children, *Why I Love Homeschooling* is the book for you. A collection of essays from a diverse group of parents: fathers, mothers, single or married, many children or one child, from all over the United States and other parts of the world. These parents talk about the many different approaches of what worked for them. I recommend this book for all parents."
— **Valerie Hollobaugh, author of *Home is Where the Learning Is*, and *Home Is Where the Learning Is For High School***

"If you're considering homeschooling, the most important thing is to hear from those who've done it. Brynn and Kathy have curated an invaluable collection of "conversations" with real people who provide practical insights into homeschooling—because they've lived it. Each story is different because each family, each student, is different. There are as many approaches to homeschooling as there are homeschoolers; that's the beauty of customized education. The conversations captured in this book will inspire and prepare you for the homeschooling journey. Reading them made me want to homeschool my kids all over again."
— **Kent Larson, author of *12 Homeschool Myths Debunked***

"This book is a valuable resource—it inspires parents to help their children make the most out of their childhood and education. It shows how parents can give their children the best education possible to help them thrive during childhood, adolescence, and beyond. I highly recommend it!"
— **Valerie Fowler, homeschool blogger, valeriefowlerwrites.com**

"This is a great book! Several of my siblings thrived more in a public school setting during high school, while I loved being homeschooled—and that's the point: One size doesn't fit all, even if it works for many. You may read one of these stories and think, "I wouldn't do things that way." That's fine—but keep reading. Because none of these stories are identical. And that's the beauty of it, because no two children are identical, either."
— **Isaac Sommers, director and founder of Ziggy Online Debate and co-founder of Integrity Communication Speech & Debate**

WHY I LOVE HOMESCHOOLING

WHY I LOVE HOMESCHOOLING

**24 PARENTS SHARE
THE JOYS & CHALLENGES OF
EDUCATING THEIR CHILDREN AT HOME**

BRYNN STEIMLE & KATHY OAKS

INFLUENCE
PRESS

First paperback edition printed July 4, 2020

www.BrynnSteimle.com/WhyILoveHomeschoolingBook

Published by Influence Press

CONTENTS

INTRODUCTION

by Brynn Steimle

On Friday, March 13, 2020 (yep, Friday the 13th—I'm not superstitious, but I couldn't help but notice), life dramatically changed in the town in Massachusetts where I live, and across the United States. That day, President Donald Trump declared a national state of emergency due to coronavirus (COVID-19). Travel bans were enacted. Social distancing guidelines were put in place—Americans were told to stay at home, or if we had to leave home, to stay six feet away from other people. Many Americans panicked. Toilet paper, hand sanitizer, soap, and face masks were in short supply, if they were available at all. Sports leagues canceled the remainder of their seasons. Churches, museums, theaters, libraries, and many other facilities closed.[1]

Then there were the school cancellations. Schools in our area were closed for one week, which was extended to three weeks, and eventually it was announced that schools would remain closed for the rest of the school year. Ultimately, most schools around the world closed, affecting more than 1.5 billion students.[2]

Many businesses throughout the world also closed their doors, sending their employees home.

Suddenly, parents and children were home together all day every day. This abrupt and unexpected change leading to forced "homeschooling," dubbed "pandemic schooling" or "crisis schooling," dramatically altered the day-to-day lives of both parents and children. Many of those parents and children struggled to adapt, and even celebrities weren't immune. Halle Berry said that pandemic schooling was a "nightmare," while Drew Barrymore said she cried all day, every day.[3]

However, many parents found they enjoyed the change—cherishing the extra time with their kids and greater involvement in their learning. This led many parents to seriously consider educating their kids at home beyond the pandemic.

As a mom who has been homeschooling my kids for years, I have experimented with many different types of homeschooling in multiple countries. I understand the immense joys that homeschooling can bring to individuals and families, and I also understand the challenges homeschooling parents face. Because of my experience, I felt I had an important contribution to make through sharing the lessons I have learned over the years. I also knew that there are many other amazing, wise homeschooling parents with important perspectives to share.

I invited Kathy Oaks to join me as a co-editor, and together, we invited a diverse group of homeschooling parents to share their experiences of homeschooling with you. They have shared the parts of homeschooling that they love, the parts that are difficult, and the lessons they've learned along the way. The twenty-four families who have shared their perspectives come from a variety of backgrounds, circumstances, and approaches to homeschooling. We've included writers of various ethnicities, religions (or lack thereof), marital statuses, and levels of education. Not everyone has chosen to identify themselves as belonging to a particular group, so it may not be obvious by reading their bio or essay. But this book is intended for parents from all backgrounds. No matter your situation, you'll find insights you can relate to and learn from.

These brave and dedicated families have given you an open invitation into their lives—come on in and see what homeschooling is like for them!

It is my hope that, if homeschooling is the right path for your family, this book will give you the encouragement and inspiration you need to jump in (or continue) with confidence.

Blessings,

Brynn Steimle

---

[1] "Updated: Timeline of the Coronavirus," *Think Global Health,* accessed at https://www.thinkglobalhealth.org/article/updated-timeline-coronavirus on June 20, 2020.

[2] "COVID-19 Impact on Education," UNESCO, accessed at https://en.unesco.org/covid19/educationresponse on June 20, 2020.

[3] "Kristen Bell, Halle Berry and More Celeb Parents Get Real About Homeschooling amid Coronavirus Pandemic," *People,* accessed at https://people.com/parents/celebrities-home-schooling-stories-coronavirus-pandemic/ on June 20, 2020.

AUTHOR'S NOTE

Homeschooling is not about trying to reproduce a school environment at home. It's not hours and hours sitting at a desk with a parent or in front of an online class. Homeschooling is about creating an environment outside of the school structure that fosters a love of learning, creativity, family closeness, and flexibility. There is no one size that fits all in homeschooling; every family is different, and approaches homeschooling in their own unique way.

Homeschooling doesn't have to be isolating—it's important to seek out and interact with others who can relate to what day-to-day life is like for you. The parents who have shared their stories in this book did so with the hope that they would provide you with much-needed support. But you and your children will greatly benefit as you seek out homeschoolers who live nearby, as well as online friends. Regardless of what kind of homeschooling you're interested in, from homeschooling with a formal structure to relaxed unschooling, from religious to secular education, there are many home-schoolers out there interested in the same things. If you cannot find homeschoolers like you who live nearby, there are plenty of online home-schooling groups. If you cannot find a group that is a good fit for your family, it's easy to create one in this digital age.

We hope this book encourages and inspires you on your homeschool journey, and expands your ideas about the concept of education and what is possible for yourselves and your children.

DISCLAIMER

The views expressed in the essays of this book are the opinions of the individual essay authors, and do not necessarily reflect the views of the book editors. Efforts have been made to include a diverse group of contributors to communicate a variety of perspectives. The content provided by the book contributors represents their personal views and is not intended to promote or malign any particular style of homeschooling, religion, ethnic group, organization, company, or individual.

WHY I LOVE HOMESCHOOLING

"Be of good cheer. Do not think of today's failures, but of the success that may come tomorrow. You have set yourselves a difficult task, but you will succeed if you persevere; and you will find a joy in overcoming obstacles. Remember, no effort that we make to attain something beautiful is ever lost."

— *Helen Keller*

1

Brynn Steimle

Brynn and her husband Josh have three children, ages ten, twelve, and fourteen—one by birth, one by adoption as a newborn, and one by international adoption at the age of thirteen. They have been home educating their children since 2014. Brynn is a children's book author, former organizer of the Hong Kong Homeschool Meetup Group, and has taught university Family Science classes. She is a member of The Church of Jesus Christ of Latter-day Saints and has a master's degree in Marriage, Family, and Human Development from Brigham Young University. She currently resides in the Boston, Massachusetts area.

ABOUT OUR FAMILY

When our oldest child was two years old, the hot topic of conversation in our toddler playgroup was making plans for preschool. The social current pushed me in the direction of preschool, but something about it didn't sit right with me. The thought of sending my young daughter away for all those hours every week, to teachers whose values I didn't know, didn't appeal to me. I also knew there wasn't anything a preschool teacher could teach her that I couldn't teach her at home. I wasn't worried about socialization if she didn't go to preschool because she spent plenty of time playing with cousins and kids from our neighborhood, she and I attended a weekly parent-child Kindermusik class, and she went to classes with her peers at church every Sunday.

Instead of enrolling our daughter in preschool, we opted out.

As our daughter neared kindergarten age, my husband and I asked ourselves, "Why can't we keep doing what we're doing?" And we began to research homeschooling our kids long-term. I didn't have any close friends or neighbors who homeschooled, but I read books, talked to the few homeschoolers I knew, and dropped in on homeschool park days to talk to other homeschooling parents. The more I researched homeschooling the more it appealed to me. But the prospect of homeschooling was also daunting, overwhelming, and downright scary! There's very little in this world more important to me than my children's education. Could I really take on such a huge responsibility?

However, I was highly motivated to make it work. The words of one homeschooler I spoke to stuck with me: "My kids will be eighteen and gone from home before I know it. I cherish the time I have with them." I felt that way too! Little by little, I gained the confidence I needed to continue to homeschool our daughter for kindergarten and beyond.

Then everything changed. When our kids were five and three, we moved to Hong Kong. Immersion in Chinese language and culture was something we couldn't provide at home. And the opportunity to send our daughter to a Chinese kindergarten seemed too good to pass up, especially since we knew we would be adopting an older Chinese child.

We found a kindergarten that came highly recommended by other expats. When we met with the principal she was kind, and we liked that she was Montessori trained. However, the experience was not what we hoped it would be. Our daughter was miserable. She resisted going to school almost every day, often in tears. After school, much of her time was focused on homework and preparing for school the next day, which furthered her unhappiness. And on top of the struggles, she didn't even learn Chinese.

The rest of the family was also miserable. Our daughter's school schedule and homework assignments seemed to take over our lives. We felt like we were making large sacrifices with little return. When we realized the stomach problems our daughter had developed were linked to the anxiety caused by attending school, that was the last straw. With one month left in the school year, we pulled her out and commenced "deschooling." All of us were happier, and our daughter's natural love of learning gradually returned. When we moved to China a couple years later, and then back to the United States in 2019, we continued to homeschool.

The daughter I mentioned above is now twelve, our son (who has always homeschooled) is ten, and during the summer of 2019, we adopted our oldest daughter from China—she is fourteen.

We hoped our new daughter would like homeschooling, but it was difficult for her to adapt. Prior to the adoption, she had spent three years at a boarding school in China, all day, seven days a week, with a high degree of structure. In our home, she struggled to adapt to the more flexible, partially self-directed, learning environment.

After five months of homeschooling, our new daughter requested to be enrolled in school, and we agreed. But after less than two months, school was canceled due to COVID-19. She is now home with us and has expressed an interest in homeschooling in the future.

WHAT I LOVE ABOUT HOMESCHOOLING

For me, the best part of homeschooling is the time I get to spend with my kids. I especially love reading aloud with them each day. We get comfy on the couch, and sometimes while I read, the kids will hold a pet or occupy their hands with slime, kinetic sand, or an art or craft project. I read picture books—yes even to my fourteen-year-old—as well as classic literature, contemporary middle-grade books, etc. We have formed many beautiful shared memories and have learned so much by enjoying good books together.

There are many other things I love about homeschooling. A few of them include freedom and flexibility, the ability to follow my children's learning timetables, direct involvement in my children's learning, and positive socialization.

Freedom and Flexibility

When I first started homeschooling, I expected it to be stressful and difficult. But I was shocked to find that it was much less stressful for me (not to mention my daughter) than sending her to half-day kindergarten. When she was in school, our family schedule was held captive by her school schedule. That schedule altered wake-up times, meal times, and bedtimes for the whole family. It also affected how much time we had together as a family in the evening, since she had difficult, often tear-inducing homework every night. And the school's schedule dictated when our family could take vacations or travel with my husband on his business trips. Homeschooling gives our family a freedom that feels so natural.

A few years ago, when I struggled with some health challenges and often needed to stay in bed all day, it was no problem. My kids and I watched lots of educational shows and read books together. Our bed-schooling time is a good memory for us.

Homeschooling also minimizes stress and anxiety. My oldest daughter's middle school only allowed a four-minute break between classes and a twenty-five-minute break for lunch. All day long she was rushed from one class to another with barely enough time to get a drink or go to the restroom. The free time provided by homeschooling allows kids to breathe and to live life at a gentle pace, while still getting plenty done.

My husband's mother was an elementary school teacher for almost two decades. In the evenings, she would share stories with the family about what happened each day. It was clear from those stories that much of her school day was taken up shuffling kids from one room to another, dealing with class clowns, and general crowd control. Homeschoolers avoid many of these distractions and get more individualized attention, which means the hours spent learning can be more productive. What takes a child six or more hours at school can often be accomplished in only an hour or two at home. The resulting free time allows kids the space to play, create, innovate, and experiment. Our kids have time to read and think. They have time to play games with their siblings or explore the backyard and woods behind our house. Free time makes room for kids to dream about their future and exercise their creativity. It's hard to come up with new ideas if your time is always scheduled.

Having more free time allows my kids to pursue their interests more deeply. My oldest daughter paints and creates other art, studies English, reads books, and keeps tabs on Chinese pop culture by watching Chinese TV shows and communicating with her friends there.

My middle daughter, who is passionate about horses, spends two to four hours every weekday working on a neighboring farm with more than twenty horses. Not only does her time at the farm provide exercise and lessons in math and science, she is also learning the value of hard work, cooperation, and responsibility. As an added bonus, her work with the horses gives her lots of ideas for a chapter book series, *The Adventures of Lena Lou*, that she and I are writing together and plan to publish.

My son loves skateboarding. In addition to keeping him physically fit, it helps him see that hard work and diligence pay off. His interest in skateboarding extends beyond the activity itself and it has pushed him to learn about video editing, art, carpentry, and entrepreneurship. We've also leveraged his interest in skateboarding to teach him basic skills—spelling and writing lessons are suddenly more interesting if you're writing out the names of professional skateboarders like Tony Hawk and Jeff Grosso. Because we homeschool we're able to travel around to skateparks in the area during the day, when they're not so crowded. Increased time and access, along with setting goals, have allowed him to progress rapidly and boosted his confidence. Since he began skateboarding, he's a much happier kid.

As homeschoolers, my kids have the freedom to pursue their dreams as a central part of their education.

Direct Involvement in My Children's Learning

When my daughters attended school (one in kindergarten and the other in eighth grade), communication from their teachers about what they were learning was rare. After school when I asked my daughters what they learned, more often than not they replied, "I don't know." It felt unnatural for me to be so removed from their learning, but as a homeschooling parent, I'm aware of and involved in what my kids are learning.

Also, I love learning alongside my kids, and I love that my kids learn many things together, even though they're all different ages. We have family discussions about what we learn, which would be more difficult if everyone was in school being forced to learn certain mandated subjects, rather than being able to choose a lot of what they learn.

Some kids are ready to learn to read when they're three years old, and others aren't ready until nine or ten. Some kids can memorize the multiplication table when they're seven, and some aren't ready until much later. Kids who aren't ready to learn something when the school dictates they should are often made to feel unintelligent, which can impede their long-term development. Homeschooling has allowed me to customize my children's education to fit how slowly or quickly they learn.

Socialization

Homeschooling enables our kids to avoid the negative socialization which is common in many schools, and allows us to expose them to much more positive experiences.

I attended public schools in seven different cities around the U.S., and American schools in Asia and Europe. My husband attended several public and private schools in California. Between the two of us, some examples of the negative socialization that happened at our schools include the following:

- Kids making fun of other kids who took learning seriously.
- Kids cheating and pressuring others to cheat.
- Kids being excluded because they didn't fit in.

- Bullying of all types. (These days, smartphones with cameras and social media allow bullies to go much further.)
- Kids describing graphic sexual acts, starting in fourth grade.
- Fistfights (some racially motivated) on the school bus, on the playground, and inside the school.
- A gang shooting.
- Kids using and dealing hard drugs at school and on field trips, beginning in fourth grade.
- Frightening and even physically dangerous behavior by a teacher, with no recourse for parents and students.
- Teachers condoning and encouraging behavior we consider to be immoral.

In 2004, the U.S. Department of Education reported that almost ten percent of students in the U.S. will become victims of teacher or other school staff sexual misconduct by the time they graduate from high school.[1] This doesn't include student-on-student sexual misconduct. It is also widely accepted that incidents of sexual assault are underreported.

When people find out that our family homeschools, they often ask, "What about socialization?" Yes, that's a major reason why we homeschool. The fundamental unit of society is the family, not the classroom, and the antisocial behavior common at schools interferes with preparing our children to raise happy and healthy families of their own. Our kids have their fair share of arguments with each other, and one of my kids often pesters and teases the other two, but that's the extent of it. There is a very low risk of any of the above examples of negative socialization happening.

Yes, kids need to learn how to deal with negative influences, difficult situations, and exposure to temptations, but that's not what I see taught at schools today. In many instances, what my husband and I consider to be antisocial behavior is taught as acceptable, even desirable, at school, by students and staff alike. Even if we endorsed everything taught in schools, placing five- or six-year-old kids into situations with large class sizes and only one or two teachers to supervise, redirect, and guide the children, is not the ideal situation for children to learn how to cope with the above challenges. I can't help but wonder how much extreme antisocial behavior in society could be avoided through homeschooling.

At a time when young people are living with their parents longer, getting married later, and struggling to create successful families, homeschooling provides the kind of positive socialization that helps children grow into self-reliant, confident, healthy adults. My husband and I treasure the unique opportunity we have to assist our children in their transition to adulthood. Homeschooling allows us to supervise and guide our children every day, as they work, learn, and play together. They learn how to resolve conflicts, treat each other with respect, and serve one another. "No other success in life can compensate for failure in the home,"[2] and homeschooling provides an environment where we can make family the priority, while also preparing our children for their future professional, family, and civic lives.

Schools divide children into same-age groups and teach them to obey an authority figure who stands at the front of the room. This isn't a common arrangement outside of school. When I think of people working together on a project at a business, arguing before a judge in a court of law, or serving in a community, I see more parallels with family life than school life.

When it comes to the matter of socializing with people outside our family, our kids have plenty of opportunities. We attend homeschool meetups, my kids work with other kids and adults at the horse farm, and we get together with friends with similar interests. My kids participate in extracurricular classes and activities, and in a church youth group. They regularly associate with kids who are homeschooled and kids who are not. My kids also often help me grocery shop and run other errands where they interact with adults of all ages.

One final benefit of homeschooling is that when we move, our kids don't have to adjust to a new school or a new curriculum. My two kids that

I raised from birth have lived in five different neighborhoods in three different countries. When we move, learning happens in a different place (our new home), but other than that, everything stays the same, educationally speaking. Homeschooling adds stability to their lives amid all the change.

HOMESCHOOLING CHALLENGES

I love homeschooling. And my kids prefer it, too. But there are days when things don't go well and I feel like throwing in the towel and shipping them off to school the next day. Most of the challenges fall into one of three categories—the kids lacking motivation, alone time for me, and making friends, for both me and my kids.

Motivation

Because my kids homeschool and we choose not to participate in an academic co-op, they don't have the constant pressure to measure up to their peers academically. I have distinct memories of learning multiplication in second grade and being motivated to learn because I wanted to keep up with my classmates. Two of my kids, on the other hand, have zero internal motivation to master multiplication and relatively little peer pressure. In most ways, avoiding the peer pressure and competition so pervasive in a school setting is great! But when it comes to being motivated to be proficient in certain areas, it comes with its own difficulties. We address this challenge by trying to inspire and motivate them through educational games, books they enjoy, shows about talented or driven people, and mentors.

Alone Time for Me

Even though my husband works from home and our youngest is now ten, it's still hard to make time for exercise, running errands without the kids, and alone time (which is especially important for introverts like me). It was even more difficult when the kids were younger. It is possible and we've made it work, but it requires intentional coordination and prioritization.

Making Friends

Homeschooling can add challenges for both parents and kids when it comes to making friends. When we lived in Hong Kong, my daughter made friends through school, and I made friends with their parents at the daily drop-off and pickup. We lived in a "no cars allowed" community, so everyone walked and biked everywhere, and it was easy to stop and talk, which made making friends a lot easier. When we switched to homeschooling we maintained those relationships. If we wanted to do something during the day with other families, though, we had to find families who were homeschooling, and there weren't many on the island where we lived. I organized a homeschooler gymnastics class and later a drama class, but attending these classes required us to take a ten-minute bike ride, then a forty-minute bus ride, and finally a fifteen-minute walk. Often we had to ride our bikes and wait for the bus in pouring rain or stifling heat (frequently both). It was a challenge, but it was worth it, and we made lifelong friends.

When we moved to Shenzhen, China there were even fewer homeschoolers than there were in Hong Kong, and the expat community was much smaller. It was easy to feel isolated.

Now, it's great living in the Boston area with co-ops, homeschool meetups, and homeschool social groups galore. But since we don't live in a cul-de-sac and our kids don't go to the bus stop every day with other kids, it's been hard to get to know kids who live nearby. It takes a bit of effort.

The reality is that no matter what form of education you pursue for your child, there will be challenges. But for our family, the benefits of homeschooling far outweigh the difficulties.

PARTING WORDS

I remember a playground conversation with another mom when I was living in Hong Kong. "You don't choose easy, do you?" She said this after learning that we were homeschooling our kids and planning to adopt an older child from China.

The question led me to ponder my life choices. No, choosing the easiest route has never been my top priority. Doing what is right for my family, even if it breaks from the status quo, is more important to me than choosing easy. Rather than just going with the flow, I value creating what the leading family therapist and researcher William Doherty calls an *intentional family*.[3]

Taking an unorthodox approach to education and life has its challenges, but doing what is best for our family is always worth whatever challenges we face in the process. I remind myself regularly, as my former professor Jeffrey Hill used to say again and again in talking about taking on challenges in family life—"It's a hard thing, but you can do hard things!"[4]

Life feels so much more meaningful and so much more fulfilling when my husband and I intentionally and prayerfully decide and then follow through with doing what is best for our family. And for now, homeschooling is what we feel is best for our family. I'm grateful for this path we are on. I'm grateful that my husband and I, on a daily basis, are able to be actively involved in our children's education and upbringing.

When people ask me about homeschooling, I tell them what a wise homeschooling mama once told me: "My kids will be eighteen and gone from home before I know it. I cherish the time I have with them!"

---

[1] U.S. Department of Education, "Educator Sexual Misconduct: A Synthesis of Existing Literature," *PPSS* 2004-09. Accessed at https://www2.ed.gov/rschstat/research/pubs/misconductreview/report.pdf on June 20, 2020.

[2] J. E. McCulloch, *Home: The Savior of Civilization* (1924), 42; quoted in *Conference Report* (April, 1935), 116.

[3] William J. Doherty, *The Intentional Family: Simple Rituals to Strengthen Family Ties* (New York: HarperCollins, 1999).

[4] Hill, E. Jeffrey, "Family Crucibles: Finding Peace in Trying Times," *Marriage and Families*, 2004, Vol. 13 , Article 3.

2

KATHY OAKS

Kathy is a photographer, author, and educator who is passionate about travel and learning. She and her husband Tom live in the Midwest with their three boys, ages eight, thirteen, and sixteen. Kathy is dedicated to helping parents and kids who want to take a non-traditional approach to education. She has written three additional books on homeschooling: Homeschoolers Are Not Hermits, *to support families as they make the transition from conventional schooling to the adventure of homeschooling,* The Homeschoolers Are Not Hermits Quick Start Guide, *and* Road Schooling, *to bring her family's love of travel to others.*

ABOUT OUR FAMILY

My husband and I have three boys, ranging in age from eight to sixteen years old, and have been homeschooling from the beginning. We did try Montessori kindergarten for the older two, but it was a short-lived experiment. There was nothing wrong with the school itself, it was quite a good school. It just turned out that everyone preferred homeschooling instead.

We have a very child-led and eclectic approach to homeschooling, pulling in resources from anywhere that works for us and is affordable. Free is

13

even better. We're a bit more structured than radical unschoolers but we come from the same principle of respecting the younger set as full human beings, with valid opinions and ideas. We work with our children to figure out how best to fulfill not only their educational needs but also their emotional and social ones. And we make sure to leave them plenty of unstructured time.

Everyone has a voice in our family, and while some things are non-negotiable, like doing chores and furthering learning, the way we go about things is always negotiable. Is a workbook boring? Let's find another way to cover the subject. There are so many possibilities, from library books to videos to museums to research projects. Is Friday a really busy day with classes, either at the co-op or (currently) online? Let's drop the chores and just keep up with the dishes that day. Is it too noisy to do math during the day? Great, let's work on it after the youngest has headed to bed. We're adaptable.

Our kids are used to having only a small part of their day dedicated to formal learning and are free to spend the rest of their time engaged in whatever interests them. We model our love of learning, and it seems to have rubbed off. I catch them reading about everything from computer programming to physics to travel, plus fiction and Dungeons and Dragons (D&D) books. While they do spend time online playing video games, they also spend time connecting with their friends, learning languages, watching amusingly educational videos, and even programming video games themselves.

WHAT I LOVE ABOUT HOMESCHOOLING

I love just about everything about homeschooling, especially how close we all are to each other. Our oldest two are best friends (although it took them a little while to figure that out). Even when we have personality clashes it doesn't take too long to work through the problem, and our youngest is now old enough to start appreciating some of the same things his brothers enjoy. We all like being in each other's company. Sure, everyone needs a break from other people at times, but mostly we get along really well.

Beyond our close family bonds, my favorite things about homeschooling are what I call the three "T"s: Time, Tailoring, and Travel.

Time

Traditional school takes up lots of time. All day, in fact! School-at-home takes up almost the same amount of time, since it's usually structured similarly. Fortunately, homeschooling doesn't have to look like school, and formal learning doesn't have to take all day. Once I freed myself from the idea that I had to dictate a school-type schedule to my kids, the whole thing got a lot easier and, yes, freed up a lot of time. We were able to create a structure that worked for us, and one that changed over time as the kids matured and their interests changed.

We do enough formal learning to satisfy the state's requirements, but it certainly doesn't take seven hours a day. Then we can get to the informal parts, where the real learning begins. That includes discussing ideas and problems, reading, watching videos (we're big on history and science in our family), exploring the world, and playing games. Yes, learning through playing games is part of our homeschool. At one point our community had a weekly homeschool board game day and we never missed it unless we were out of town. Our oldest has become an accomplished classical pianist in three years because he had the time to dedicate to it without missing any schoolwork. There are so many things we've been able to do because we aren't stuck in the school structure.

Tailoring

Tailoring education to each child's individual interests, strengths, and weaknesses is another major bonus of homeschooling. Our oldest loves math and music, and we've been able to foster that while making sure he got help with his terrible spelling. He's just starting both a calculus class and his own YouTube channel to showcase his piano skills. On the other hand, his brain wasn't ready to take on chapter books until age eleven. He could

15

read, he just didn't do text-heavy books. That would have been a huge handicap in school. At home he read tons of graphic novels and listened while I read books aloud every day. I still do. When he was ready, he picked up *Harry Potter* and read the first five books in two weeks. Then he went on to reading biographies of famous mathematicians that we happened to have around the house. Yes, that's what my husband likes to read for fun, too.

Our middle son has quite different interests. He loves to read, especially fiction, and taught himself at age three. He also loves to write, and some of his homeschool projects include writing and publishing his own fiction on Amazon. Writing *real* books to publish is definitely more motivating than writing about some pre-determined subject for a class. On the other hand, he had to work harder to memorize math facts than his brother. His brain is more like mine, higher math like algebra comes much easier than remembering the multiplication table. When he stopped comparing himself to his brother he was able to understand his own way of learning better. He has also run a D&D game for several years, which has helped him learn about planning, world building, and managing groups of enthusiastic but rowdy kids. He really enjoys learning about history, and has found some great YouTube channels that we all enjoy watching together. In fact, he's sparked an interest in history in those of us who weren't already into it.

Being able to tailor an education to each kid really comes to the fore with our youngest. I can't imagine what he would have done in school. He loves electronics and computers, and taught himself to read by looking through books on Scratch programming and on building electronic circuits. Instead of buying expensive curricula, we bought him a Raspberry Pi computer to build himself (with help from Dad) at age six. Now he has three. Also in kindergarten he built a working radio from Snap Circuits and an electronic breadboard and a scavenged speaker—without any help. I heard a funky crackling noise and went to see what he was up to, and there he was tuning in to a station on a mishmash of circuits. He discusses logarithmic functions at bedtime with Dad, and takes apart anything we're done with. And a few things we're not! But he has terrible spelling and handwriting, and has forgotten his multiplication table again, and needs to move constantly whenever he's not concentrating on something. He wouldn't enjoy sitting in a classroom, and I suspect they wouldn't enjoy having him there.

Travel

Travel is my other most favorite thing about homeschooling. These days, travel isn't so easy, but we've been taking road trips for ten years now. Homeschooling allows us to go during the off season, and the homeschooling mindset lets us make road trips into fun and educational experiences. We've been working our way through the National Parks on our way to see the relatives every year, and we've even started making forays into other countries. One of the best things about having no separation between life and learning is that the kids are happy to be learning all the time. Travel isn't a vacation from learning. Instead, it's a time to immerse ourselves in geography and history and culture. We don't need to get permission from the school to grab an opportunity to travel, travel is an integral part of our homeschool experience.

HOMESCHOOLING CHALLENGES

Homeschooling isn't without its challenges. I think the biggest one we've dealt with has been the differences in age range and interests. The two oldest boys, even with a three-year gap in between them, have become fast friends. As soon as they were able to play with LEGOs together and enjoy each other's company, they've been great. Although they have different talents, it hasn't made much difference in their ability to get along and find games and movies and friends that they both like. The five-year gap when our youngest came along has proved more difficult to bridge. His intense interest in computers has also been a barrier, since his brothers weren't interested in programming or building computers or radios.

That gap has closed somewhat as they've all gotten older. They all are interested in programming now, and give each other advice on their various programs. They also like sharing ideas on LEGO creations and seeing the interesting things the others have made. They are finding more common ground in other interests these days, including games and videos. But the older and younger set have very different groups of friends, and still don't have as much in common. On the other hand, the two older boys now are quite self-sufficient and can get much of their learning and socializing done with minimal supervision. That lets me spend more individual time with our youngest, which we both enjoy.

The other major challenge that I've found has been in documenting our work. To be honest, I burned out. I kept a journal—one of those week-at-a-glance calendars—for years. Every night I wrote down what we'd done that day, breaking it down into things like reading, math, science, socialization, fine motor, health, etc. If we watched "Schoolhouse Rock" or "The Electric Company" that got put down. If we baked together, I wrote it in. If we went on a nature walk with friends, that was included. I wrote down everything I read out loud and whatever I saw them reading. It was really helpful in those early years, whenever I second-guessed myself and wondered if we really should be doing more formal schooling. I could look back at everything we'd done over the past few months and see that we were indeed covering a whole lot of ground, even if it didn't look like "work." I have a box of these journals.

Now, when I really should be keeping track of all that information to make sure I can fill out high school transcripts easily, I can't seem to do it. I go back and look at what we've done and fill it in afterwards, but I'm sure I'm missing plenty of books and activities. I finally have given up on journals and am not going to buy one this year. The last two have only sporadic entries. It's really something of a relief to not write every single thing down. I'm glad the older boys are taking math classes and doing more formal coursework that is already documented for me.

Those aren't the only challenges we've faced, but no life is without challenges. Challenges faced with a growth mindset can bring out the best in us. I hope that the boys are learning to deal with adversity as we navigate through them. To me, handling tight budgets and dealing with naysaying relatives and finding good homeschool groups are totally worth managing for the benefits of homeschooling. In fact, I had to think a lot longer to come up with challenges I wanted to discuss for this essay than I did for the benefits. I even quizzed the kids to get their opinions, and they felt the same. The benefits so far outweigh the disadvantages that for us it's no contest at all.

PARTING WORDS

If you think homeschooling might be the way to go, I urge you to give it a try. Spend some time deschooling, to get the whole family out of the "school" mindset, and approach homeschooling with the idea that learning should be enjoyable. Yes, it might require effort, but it shouldn't be forced or tedious or even humiliating. I had plenty of humiliating moments in school, as did most people I know. It can be harder for us adults to get past the way we were indoctrinated through the school system than it is for kids. For some insights into that indoctrination, check out John Taylor Gatto's speech (and essay) titled *Dumbing Us Down*. I also highly recommend reading John Holt's book *Growing Without Schooling* to start thinking about all the possibilities.

Remember, nothing is written in stone here. You have the freedom to work with your kids to figure out the very best way to educate them. That will be different for every family, and most likely for every child. If it works best to do formal learning in the evenings after work, do that. If it works best to send one child to school and homeschool another, do that. If it works best to have one child doing open-ended projects while another needs the structure of online classes, do that. And if it stops working, talk together and figure out what to do next. Things are constantly changing around our house, and I check in with the kids fairly often to discuss how we could make things go more smoothly. I like to tackle small problems before they fester and become big ones. Our solutions have to work for the whole family, including the adults, even if they're not ideal.

I'd like to leave you with a quote from our eight-year-old. He said, "What I like best about homeschooling is trying things out to see if they work." He was referring to his computer and electronics projects, but I think it really applies to the whole homeschooling experience. Have fun trying out new things and figuring out what works for your family.

3

DAN ARCHIBALD

Dan and his wife Leah share a house with three boys, two dogs, and an ever-changing number of chickens (well, the chickens aren't usually in the house). Besides hanging out with the boys, Dan is a Kids Church Pastor at Reservoir Church in Cambridge, Massachusetts, a part-time role, and spends time gardening, baking, building things, and exploring the local woods and swamps. He studied history at Cornell and has a Master's in Elementary Education from The University of Massachusetts Lowell. He worked in public schools for several years. Dan is an organizer of the Assabet River Home-school Co-op and blogs at www.squibix.net.

ABOUT OUR FAMILY

I sometimes tell people that we fell into homeschooling by accident. Our oldest was still four the year we got a kindergarten registration packet in the mail for the first time. He would have been one of the youngest kids in his class, we didn't feel like kindergarten would be that good for him, and we enjoyed having him around . . . so we kept him home. That year we just kept on doing the same kinds of things we'd always done together as a family, and it was fine. Then when the new school year arrived we wanted

21

to stick with that routine, so we filed a home education plan like the state wanted us to. The next thing we knew, we were homeschooling three boys age ten, eight, and five! Amazing.

Only that's not really the real story. And anyone who sends their kids to school can probably spot the clues in that first paragraph. Like, why didn't our son go to preschool? How did we ever think that "just keeping him home" was an option? And why on earth did we want to?! Really, our thoughts about the childhood we hoped he could have were non-standard from the beginning. And that's despite the fact that I'm trained in Elementary Education and worked in public schools.

WHAT I LOVE ABOUT HOMESCHOOLING

One important reason we home educate is that we like being with our kids. We've been lucky enough to have flexible work schedules to make that happen—my wife, Leah, was home when the first two boys were little, then we each worked part time for the "preschool" years, and now she's working full time while I hold things down at home. I enjoy doing things with my kids, and I want to make sure that they're able to do the things that they find important and valuable. Also, we don't want to waste their time! I'm 100% committed to the existence of public schooling as a public good, and I think most public school teachers are fantastic people—but schools require kids to be there in that building for six or seven hours a day to get maybe an hour of relevant instructional time. It's better for them to be free of those walls.

Our home education is shaped by two sometimes competing impulses. First is our belief that kids are human beings with an inbuilt drive to learn, and with the capacity—and right!—to make many decisions for themselves. (I keep John Holt's *How Children Learn* and Agnes Leistico's *I Learn Better By Teaching Myself* on the bookshelf above my desk to remind myself of that when I start to get stressed out.) I recognize that a big part of learning comes through play: For example, I've had moments of despair at failed attempts to get my kids writing, but then I notice them playing with little figures and narrating a complex, multi-character story. Learning also needs to be driven by genuine interest: Nobody can learn something they don't care about.

At the same time, though, I am trained as a teacher and sometimes I like teaching things. So I don't think you could really call us unschoolers. A few days a week we have some organized instructional time, all together or one-on-one. Some weeks it's every day! Sometimes there are even worksheets. But that more formal work is always conditional on the kids' voluntary engagement: I try to make it explicit that they don't have to participate if they're not interested (though sometimes the frustration in my voice when I say it undercuts the message—something I have to work on!). In my more self-aware moments I call our less-inspired instructional time "playing school" and recognize that, at best, it's giving the kids tools to do their own learning later. But sometimes it brings real engagement in the moment. Like this week when our study of reproduction and genetics led to the creation of a pencil-and-paper game that had us breeding monsters for the next two days.

I think what I love most about home education is flexibility. When it's rainy and there's nothing to do, we can read books together and talk about them. Maybe something in a book will inspire us to do some drawing. Or maybe we'll just play a board game. On sunshiny days anyone who wants to can be outside for hours, observing—even if only in passing and by accident—the natural world. Sometimes math instruction is practicing times tables (is there any way to learn basic multiplication facts except by doing them over and over?), but sometimes it's building a picnic table and calculating the angle to cut the pieces for the legs. How many degrees are in a triangle? I'm not good at planning, so I'm happy to come up with a general idea—talking about reproduction, say—and see where it takes us.

I also feel that it's incredibly valuable for my kids to be able to learn as individuals. Even beyond their particular interests, which they may or may not be able to develop in a school setting, school norms would force them into possibly uncomfortable boxes. Watching the three of them grow up I see that their learning and development doesn't move forward in a linear way but in fits and starts, and at different rates for each of them. Because of that, I can't think of them as a "fifth-grader," a "third-grader," and a "kindergartener," and compare them to their peers in each of those grades. Neither of my older two boys learned to read before their second-grade year, which would have meant hours and hours of separate reading instruction had they been in school; now they both spend endless time absorbed in books. And I don't even have to call that a success story: In the home education setting, not liking to read would also be fine! Home education lets each child really be themselves.

HOMESCHOOLING CHALLENGES

That's not to say there aren't challenges! Some challenges are wrapped up with the same things that attracted me to this lifestyle in the first place. Flexibility, for example, goes both ways. It can be hard to abandon my designs for the day when it's clear the kids need something else. And sometimes it's hard to come up with any ideas of what to do! If there was a plan that we had to follow—if somebody else was telling us what to do—then at least I wouldn't have to worry about coming up with all the ideas. Also, as the "education planner" in the household, I sometimes struggle with knowing when to intervene: Should I work to make sure my ten-year-old can write his numbers the right way around, or to encourage my six-year-old to use a "proper" pencil grip? If I don't teach them math am I allowing them to develop their interest in the subject naturally and organically, or am I denying them the foundation they need to discover a love of more complicated mathematics later? I don't know.

Enjoying spending time with the kids can also lead to challenges: If I didn't like being with them, I wouldn't need to work so hard to engage them! Lots of people with kids in school imagine home education means my kids are asking me what to do all the time; that is not the case. Most of the time they're happy to ignore me and do their own thing together or individually.

That dynamic also interacts with my teacher sensibilities. When I think there's something they would enjoy learning then I need to work hard to present it in a way that will draw them in. And sometimes it's a complete bust anyway! It's discouraging to come up with what I think is a fascinating project or outing that, when offered, doesn't elicit anything more than a vague "no thanks" from behind a book. On the other side of the coin, sometimes it's hard for me to see value in what they're choosing to do because it's different than what I would choose. Screen time, for example, is an ongoing issue in our house that hasn't yet been entirely resolved by democratic and non-coercive means.

There's also some stress around other people's expectations. People asking if our six-year-old is reading, for example, or offering pointed questions about "socialization." Not to mention reporting and state standards! A few years ago, for my annual progress report to the school district, I sent in a writing sample for my oldest son. He had worked so hard on the skills it took to be able to write out an entire page, and I was so proud of him. In the letter we got back from the school district, the only personalized note—the only personalized response we've ever received in four years of reporting—was a suggestion to look into tools for online spelling practice. Sometimes all those expectations get to me, and I find myself saying things to the kids like, "I know you don't want to, but you absolutely must produce something that the state will see as learning." That's dumb, right?

Because, really, I know that they're learning all the time (even if I sometimes need John Holt to remind me). They learned to ride bikes, to swim, to draw and write comic books, to wash dishes, to make jigsaw puzzles, to know when to walk away from a friend who's making bad choices. And I didn't teach them any of that! Although I did offer tips on the jigsaw puzzles and, more pointedly, the dishes. I do get to teach them some things—about seeds and eggs, about converting fractions into decimals, about our country's history of racism, about the poems that I love. Put it all together, and it's totally worth it. In our house, education isn't something that happens somewhere else, separate from the rest of our life. It's just another part of everything we do together as we work, play, relax, and adventure together. And I love it!

PARTING WORDS

Should everyone have their kids learn at home? Lots of the time I think that, yes, of course they should! But I also think that everyone should keep chickens and travel by bicycle and listen to weird music and go to bed when it gets dark. My personal preferences, that is to say, are sometimes idiosyncratic. I recognize that for many people the reality of jobs and schedules means that there's no time to think about organizing home education. That's fine! Despite some strong words above, I think public school is a great option. I liked most of my own time there, both as a student and as a teacher. But when parents tell me, "I could never teach my own kids!" I have to disagree. If you want to, you can! You're already teaching them all the most important things in their lives. And all the rest—math, history, science—is just learning together!

4

CARRIE POMEROY

Carrie has published articles, essays, and stories in Literary Mama, Life Learning, The St. Paul Almanac, *and the anthology* Riding Shotgun: Women Write About Their Mothers, *among other places. An avid library volunteer and community activist, she lives with her husband and their son, seventeen, and their daughter, fourteen, in St. Paul, Minnesota.*

ABOUT OUR FAMILY

A few weeks ago, my daughter asked if I'd help her declutter the attic of our century-old house in St. Paul. A longtime Irish dancer, she's been doing dance classes via Zoom since COVID-19 hit and using the attic as a practice studio. Being the only neat freak in our family of four, it was starting to bother her how messy it was up there. So over the course of a few weekends, we dove in.

Sifting through layers of old toys like archeologists on a dig site, we took a trip back to her early childhood. We unearthed the LEGO DUPLOs that she and her older brother turned into elaborate castles and amusement parks. We sorted through the Matchbox and Hot Wheels cars that the two of them created stories around, stories that could stretch for days.

When my husband and I first decided to homeschool, we both pictured playing a fairly traditional teaching role. He's a research fellow at a medical device company in a Twin Cities suburb; I'm a writer and community organizer. Between the two of us, we figured we'd have a lot of important stuff covered.

We renovated our attic into what we thought would be our home classroom. We installed cupboards for storing craft supplies and racks for displaying books and kids' magazines. We put up whiteboards.

When I told people we were planning to homeschool, they'd often say, "Good for you! I could never do that. I just don't have the patience."

I fully believed my husband and I *did* have the patience to teach our kids at home: the patience to teach them how to write, how to read, how to do math, and how to make sense of the world around them.

I had no idea just how much homeschooling would challenge my patience, in ways I never expected. Here's our family's homeschooling story, a story of a different kind of patience.

WHAT I LOVE ABOUT HOMESCHOOLING

In my early days of homeschooling, I tried to do what I thought I was supposed to do as a homeschooling mom and act like a traditional classroom teacher. I vividly remember the day I decided that we should make red and white construction paper *Cat in the Hat* hats to celebrate Dr. Seuss's birthday. My son was about three or four. I don't know who cried more, me or him. Probably me.

I quickly figured out that our homeschooling days went so much more smoothly when I stopped worrying about what kids were "supposed" to learn by a certain age and let go of trying to be my children's teacher. Instead, I tried to sit back and notice what they were interested in, then seek out library books and movies and outings that would feed whatever was making them light up at the time. And I talked with them about whatever was making *me* light up.

Those whiteboards in our attic never did get used for any formal lessons. Instead, they became menu boards for restaurants, for playing school, for keeping score in made-up games with rules that eluded me but seemed to make sense to my kids and their friends.

We never did set up a table for the kids to do schoolwork on, either. Instead, they spread out on the floor and colored or built with LEGOs while I read out loud to them. Armed with foam swords and plastic balls, they built weird ramshackle forts and waged mock battles against their dad. They created potions from ingredients they hauled up from our kitchen. They dictated stories to me while they swung on our backyard swing or paced the floor dressed in costumes from our dress-up basket.

All the while, my children *were* learning, in ways that turned my expectations about education upside-down.

My son became obsessed with Monopoly for a few months when he was six. All that buying and selling of St. James Place and Baltic Avenue taught him a surprising amount of arithmetic. A few years later, he spent hours poring over LEGO catalogs. I later realized that he was calculating how long it would take him to save his allowance for sets he wanted. He even taught himself about percentages so he'd know how much sales tax he would owe.

I sometimes worried about how much time he spent online. But he learned to type and spell because he wanted to be able to keep up in chats on a Minecraft server with his friends. He honed his ability to write persuasively, with a clear purpose and for different audiences, in online video-gaming forums and role-playing games.

I also worried quite a bit when my children were younger about how they would learn to read. But I didn't want to ruin their enjoyment of books by trying to force reading on them before they showed interest and readiness.

In the meantime, while I waited, I read to them for hours every day. We played word games and did puzzles and sang songs. Both kids taught themselves to read around age seven using *Calvin and Hobbes* and *Garfield* comics. My daughter practiced reading out loud by reading Stan and Jan Berenstain's *Bears on Wheels* to her dolls.

Within months of cracking the code, they'd jumped from picture books to material like the first Percy Jackson series with a speed and fluency that blew my mind.

As my children grew, we were able to talk honestly about what was working in our homeschooling life and what needed tweaking and adapting to meet the kids' needs.

Starting in third grade, my daughter chose to start attending a part-time, private Montessori program for homeschoolers three days a week. She stayed there for three years before returning to full-time homeschooling for a year in sixth grade when she decided that the Montessori program was no longer a good fit for her.

Starting in seventh grade, she began attending an online, project-based charter school, where she chooses what she wants to study, logs the time she spends on her projects, and determines how she'll present what she's learned to her advisor and her fellow students, whether it's through a poster, a slideshow, or a research paper.

"I want more structure," she's told me about her decision to attend school, "but I don't want it from you." I considered it a homeschooling win that she could articulate what she wanted so clearly.

My daughter's school advisor raves about how organized and motivated my daughter is and how impressed she is by her ability to reflect on what she's learning and make meaning from her experiences.

My daughter has shown great discernment about what she wants from a learning situation in other contexts. As a dancer, she's been able to walk away from dance schools where teachers didn't treat students respectfully or give them specific feedback on how to improve. She's now at a dance school where her teacher genuinely cares about her students as people and actively works to help them grow.

It's impossible to say how many of my daughter's strengths stem from her early years of homeschooling, and how many would have manifested whether she went to school or not.

But I have to think that years of her father and me asking her, "What do *you* want to do today?", of being told that she has the right to spend her days in ways that make her feel happy and fulfilled, have encouraged her not to settle for dysfunctional environments and to keep looking for environments where she can thrive.

Meanwhile, my son, who's just entering his senior year, has home-schooled throughout his education, supplementing his mostly self-directed home study with classes at a Minneapolis homeschool co-op and courses at both a local community college and the University of Minnesota.

He's been able to transition from homeschooling to college coursework with what looks to me like relative ease. He enjoys his classes, manages his workload effectively, and earns excellent grades.

It also makes me happy that he's continued to pursue independent learning even as he juggles his college course-load, devouring books about philosophy, world history, and politics not because they're required reading, but simply because he wants to. He's also still had plenty of time to hang out with friends online and in person, and to get plenty of sleep, something that's a lot harder for his peers who have to stay up late doing homework and then get up early for school. I think being able to get adequate time for sleep is one of the great unsung benefits for homeschooling teens.

HOMESCHOOLING CHALLENGES

There is so much that I have appreciated about homeschooling. But does that mean our homeschooling has been easy or perfect? Oh, heck, no—especially not when my kids were younger and I was still so unsure of where this journey would take us.

Like so many of my homeschooling friends, I experienced plenty of self-doubt. *Was I doing enough? Were my children learning what they needed to learn to lead happy, productive, healthy lives? Would they ever stop fighting?*

Our hardest days were in the coldest, darkest months of our Minnesota winters, when we were cooped up inside for days on end and tempers often flared. When the kids squabbled in normal sibling fashion, I wasn't always the most effective referee. All too often, I let intrusive thoughts rattle me: *I thought homeschooled siblings were supposed to get along better because they spend so much time together. What am I doing wrong? Are they always going to fight like this?*

At times like that, I sometimes snapped and hollered, "That's it! I can't take it anymore. You guys are going to *have* to go to school." Sometimes I even hopped on the computer and started looking up school application deadlines while the kids cried that they didn't *want* to go to school. My kids laugh and tease me about those moments now, but it sure seemed stressful for them at the time. And it felt absolutely awful to me.

If I had that time to do over, I would prioritize caring for myself a little more, so I could have the equanimity to handle the squabbling better. I would push aside the guilt I used to feel about making time for exercise and time with friends. I'd do more things to fill my tank so I could stay calmer and more grounded for my kids.

I'd seek out therapy earlier than I eventually did, too. I think I'd also work a little harder to make sure my kids got breaks from one another—and from me.

I'd also work harder to find ways for the kids to interact with and learn from a more diverse range of people. At least in Minnesota, the homeschooling community is very white, and looking back, I see now that as I focused so intently on my children and their needs and preferences, I wasn't always working as hard as I should have to get them out into more diverse parts of our community to learn from and alongside people of color.

In a multicultural country where white people need to do a much better job of following the guidance and leadership of people of color, I think it's crucial for white children like mine to learn from people who come from a wide range of backgrounds. For homeschoolers in many parts of the country, that can be more challenging, but it's definitely a goal worth pursuing.

PARTING WORDS

While my daughter and I were up in the attic sifting through all those old toys a few weeks ago, we ran across my husband's long-buried collection of multi-sided gaming dice. We remembered the hours my daughter spent sorting the dice into different patterns and groupings on the floor. She told me that back then, she was using the dice to create a make-believe society with its own social classes, political system, and rituals.

And here I'd thought this whole time that she was using those dice to learn about math.

These days, my daughter is unusually attuned to social and interpersonal dynamics and how they affect the way the world works. She follows current events with avid interest and attentiveness, and her observations on politics and power dynamics are astute and eye-opening.

I can't help but wonder how those hours she spent sorting dice into different social classes when she was six helped shape the way she thinks about the world now.

So much of the learning that has stuck with my children the most is the learning that they initiated themselves, the learning that happened when I got out of the way and just gave them space to think, observe, and *be*.

People are definitely right to assume that homeschooling requires patience. The question is, what *kind* of patience?

For me, homeschooling requires the patience to wait until my children show a readiness to learn something in their own time, rather than measuring their progress against an external academic standard that has nothing to do with them.

It requires the patience to give my kids room to air their hurt feelings and anger with me and with each other, instead of rushing to fix their conflicts and problems on *my* timetable, so *I* can be comfortable again. It's a patience I often still struggle to cultivate.

Above all, homeschooling requires the patience to trust that even when my kids spend most of their time on pursuits that aren't conventionally academic, there is often important learning, development, or rest and gestation happening, even if I don't see it right away.

A few years ago, my son's orthodontist asked him what he liked best about having his mom as his teacher. My son thought about it for a second, and then replied, "I think it's that she lets me learn things for myself."

It wasn't the answer the orthodontist expected. But I thought it summed up pretty well what our homeschooling was about.

5

TINA NAHID

Tina is a wife to her husband Nami and both a biological and adoptive mother of three children. She has homeschooled and been a stay-at-home mom since her oldest was born. Her kids are now ages nineteen, sixteen, and thirteen. Tina has published three books: Five Minute Devotions for The Homeschool Mom, Moments of Grace: Daily Reflections for the Homeschool Mom, *and* Recovering from Betrayal: A Daily Guide to Healing. *She has an M.A. in English and enjoys speaking, writing, reading, hiking, traveling, and encouraging other families on this journey. Tina and her family live in Kentucky.*

ABOUT OUR FAMILY

My background is in English writing and teaching. When I had my firstborn son, my husband and I made the decision that I would be a stay-at-home mom. This was something I had never expected I would do! And when my husband came home from work and suggested home educating our children, I looked at him as if he had grown a third eyeball in the middle of his forehead! The idea was so foreign to my mind. Yet, out of curiosity, I began to research and lo and behold, the journey of homeschooling began.

My approach to homeschooling is what I would call "relaxed and eclectic homeschooling." I have enjoyed filling our days with nature walks and field trips, following a type of daily-life-learning philosophy, especially in the elementary years. I also have been very focused on the spiritual aspect of my children's education, so I've tried to intersperse biblical teaching throughout our days. Our curriculum is eclectic, chosen from various providers, and we have often participated in homeschool co-ops as well.

WHAT I LOVE ABOUT HOMESCHOOLING

I have enjoyed so many things about our homeschooling journey. One of the greatest blessings has been the opportunity we've had to travel and take vacations during the off-season. The freedom to teach my children according to their natural bents and personalities was something I've truly enjoyed as well. The amount of time spent getting to know my children more deeply has been another blessing. Time is truly a treasure and goes so quickly. We have so many memories together.

The friendships I have made with other moms and families within the homeschool community have also been a great source of strength and joy for me, my husband, and my children. They have made strong bonds with other children and have grown together in co-op classes and social events over the years. Also, teaching my children to read was a great joy to me, as well as sharing God's Word with my children on a daily basis. These are all wonderful privileges I would never trade, and I am very thankful.

The freedom to follow my own schedule and choose my own curriculum for each of my children was also an aspect of homeschooling that I have enjoyed each year. I don't like being tied down to someone else's agenda or schedule when it comes to education, so homeschooling affords me the opportunity to tailor our family's education more specifically for each of them according to their personalities and interests. I consider this to be one of the best parts of being a homeschool family.

I also had a goal early on for my children to become independent learners by the time they were in middle school. When I saw this take place, it was a great joy. Children can learn so much when given structure and expectations. They are often able to work ahead or finish their work by mid-day and then have the rest of their day to do things they enjoy. I believe this has given them an independent spirit and has helped them manage their own time.

HOMESCHOOLING CHALLENGES

As with all callings in life, there are certainly challenges along the homeschooling path. The time you spend with your children is a blessing looking back when they are older, but the years when they are younger and more demanding can definitely be stressful and challenging. I have many memories of going into my closet or bathroom for a good cry or temper tantrum at times. Being "on duty" continually as a mother and wife is not easy. It takes quite a bit of sacrifice to undertake educating our children, and it's important to take care of ourselves as well. But self-care can easily be neglected during these years, to which I can attest. As I have gotten older, I have realized more the importance of caring for myself physically, mentally, emotionally, and spiritually, as burnout and a feeling of depletion can certainly happen.

Dealing with discipline issues and constant bickering between siblings at times is also very challenging, especially if you have any strong-willed or special-needs children in the mix. They can be high maintenance! It's definitely a challenge to juggle being both mom and teacher all in one. My husband's involvement has often helped greatly. He is a good principal who I happen to be in love with. A perfect combo!

The teen years can present some challenges as well, depending on the child's personality and needs. Adolescence can bring an array of hormones, attitudes, and decisions that we as parents must navigate. But providing a stable home environment and freedom for our teens to manage their own education and time goes a long way towards helping them in the future. The changes in our children can be challenging during this time, but the investment we make in their lives is well worth it.

PARTING WORDS

Despite the many real challenges of homeschooling, I believe it is still so worth it to follow this path. The gift of time with our children is something we will never regret. The investment into their lives we make when we educate them at home is a gift that I believe they will look back on and remember fondly. The many warm memories made together have given them positive family bonds and a strong moral compass in life. Persevering through the challenging times can make a family closer when we cling to our faith and live out our lives daily in front of our children. When they see our failures, they learn firsthand that we are not perfect and that we all need God's help in our lives. The opportunity we have to instill wisdom, knowledge, love, and hope into our children's hearts and minds, even in learning from our mistakes as parents, is truly a gift and a legacy we can leave for their entire lives.

6

REGINA MERCHANT

Regina is a middle-aged, single mom who has lived all over the United States and now resides in the Midwest with her tween daughter. Regina earned her Bachelor of Arts while studying abroad and in the U.S. She has an extensive background in communications and in several artistic disciplines. After her child experienced multiple traumas in public school, Regina became an advocate for disability rights. She's found an individualized homeschooling approach to be the most beneficial way to produce a happier, healthier kid.

ABOUT OUR FAMILY

We are a family of two, just me and my girl. My tween loves music, dolls, LEGOs, and rainbows. We both love to express ourselves through art: daily dance breaks, random singing, easy and fun stuff to do at home. I moved us from the West Coast to the Midwest a few years ago for better healthcare, since we both have disabilities. Being a single mom with health challenges means I spend far too much time dealing with medical bureaucracy and trying to make our income last. I never thought I could afford to homeschool, but it's been worth the challenge.

My girl is a project-based, kinesthetic, secular unschooler. Don't panic if that sounds like I just spoke gibberish. When I was new to homeschooling, I wouldn't have had a clue what that meant either! Don't worry; you will have time to decode these things. Distilled, what I said means that as she happens upon something which interests her, she learns best through hands-on physical experience that is not necessarily based in a religious affiliation. Having time to discover how your kid learns best is one of the loveliest gifts of homeschooling. We naturally weave education into pursuing her interests instead of following a particular method or curriculum. I recently learned that we are also "Sparkleschoolers," intentionally bringing art into our homeschooling. See? Two years in and I am still learning new stuff. But this time, it's fun.

WHAT I LOVE ABOUT HOMESCHOOLING

I love that the pressure to perform is off. The homeschoolers we know accept and appreciate kids learning at their own rates. With no grading, the playing field is level. Kids and parents have no reason to act superior or dole out condemnation. Occasionally we are rudely grilled by random folks who have been driven to a competitive frenzy by their public schools. When I feel tolerant enough to respond to this slight annoyance, they are always surprised to learn how much my daughter has progressed. Without the judgment and pressure of public school life, with its tiered systems of reward and punishment and its adversarial nature, her love of learning has returned.

Most public school teachers I know would love more time to get to know how each of their students learns best, to give them room to explore new methods and interests. But with more than twenty kids in a class, teaching to unfair testing standards and a strict schedule, they rarely get to do it. In many American public schools, teachers can lose their jobs or funding based on low overall combined test results, so they are stuck with teaching to mandated testing standards that can be racist, exclusionary, or a poor representation of a child's skills. Moreover, for families with disabilities, school testing can be profoundly impacted by those disabilities, skewing the results and how the child's education is approached in general. The good news is local/state homeschooling advocates have already navigated the process and can help you figure it out. If your state and local laws require only that you prove the test was taken, without needing to see the results, the record of your child's strengths and challenges remain private. Suddenly, there is room to make those improvements over time. When you begin homeschooling, the day-to-day learning will no longer be overseen by the school district. In your own domain, you get more time to discover what works for you and your family.

Another benefit of homeschooling is that if my daughter or I need to take time off for health reasons, there's no homework, nothing to catch up on. We can make medical appointments, get up late, and learn in our pajamas at night if we want. I love that my girl wrote and published a book, is learning French, and sings. She has a book of forty songs that she knows because her music therapy and schooling are integrated. I love that my personal experience and education are always available to her when she needs it. And when her interests exceed my abilities or desire to supply education, there is a global community of educators available to provide it.

Homeschooling has opened more doors than it has closed, by far.

HOMESCHOOLING CHALLENGES

Our journey from public school life to homeschool life has taken some major adjustment and time. We have both been trained for many, many years by the public school system to respond to a rigorous structure with a stodgy, linear methodology. As a kid raised by public school teachers to believe that learning must be steady and reliable or something was wrong, I sometimes doubt this new path. By comparison, our schooling efforts might seem disorganized and inconsistent to some people. But here's the hopeful part. Anyone who has been present for even a little of their children's development knows that growth is naturally unpredictable and not necessarily linear. Development may stall, regress, or jump ahead, in fits and starts. So we must adapt to the terrain as we discover it.

Letting go of societal expectations is an ongoing practice. But when I do, we both become more confident and comfortable working together toward whatever her future may hold. This flexible approach meets her development wherever it is at the moment and reduces her anxiety. And her overall progress has actually accelerated.

As a disabled mom of a disabled kid, when I was considering homeschooling, I panicked over the idea of losing a variety of school-based supports. I am not a legal representative or special needs educator, but as far as I understand it, in the United States, homeschoolers are still entitled to FAPE (Free Appropriate Public Education) under IDEA (Individuals with Disabilities Education Act). Homeschoolers have varied experiences with public school-based disability education support. Check with your local homeschooling advocacy groups to see what state law says about maintaining those supports. Some have great school districts who will liaise with them to find a plan that allows for onsite or home-based support.

Your school district may or may not wish to engage in the conversation or comply with a plan. While my daughter attended public school from kindergarten through second grade, I fought school districts in two different states for years to get an Individualized Education Program (IEP) which would legally require her school to provide specific testing-based support. There is another option. And you should take a slow deep breath before you read it. Ok, here goes. . . . You might be able to let go of that IEP and use non-school-based supports for your child.

All that time and those tears (including my own) made it a tough choice to let go of having an IEP. But even with local support agencies attending meetings with me, and state agencies telling me how to phrase requests effectively, the battle to have her needs acknowledged was disheartening at best and traumatic at worst. Second-graders should never be left screaming in their lockers out of fear and struggle. As we homeschool she has slowly released the stigma of forced education from an environment never suited to her. You can learn more specifically about our challenging path through to homeschooling in my article, *Relief Is Everything: The Homeschooling Journey of a Special Needs Family.*[1] I initially wrote the article using the term "special needs" before I learned to use the term "disabled" instead. I try to follow Maya Angelou's advice: When I know better, I do better.

So how can I possibly afford to stay home and get support for her education?

First, let's acknowledge how many parents regularly lose jobs due to navigating a world not designed to accommodate disabled humans. Schedules are constantly upended by those dreaded and unpredictable school calls for the parent to immediately pick up their child. Multiple doctor appointments are scheduled according to the doctors' availability without regard to the family's schedule. Health emergencies create upset and delays. Add on the endless medical paperwork to both the upkeep and breakdowns of cross-communication among parents, care providers, schools, and therapists. There is no way to keep all those balls in the air and get it all done, including keeping a job. To quote a good friend, "I drop more balls than I ever catch."

In order to afford to homeschool my daughter, I was compelled to alter my approach. In some locations, state waivers may cover therapies and make pay available to parents who provide care for qualifying children who exceed the need for standard parenting care. When children are unable to independently manage standard activities of daily living, they may require nursing or behavioral support. Check with a county caseworker and other local parents of disabled kids. You may be entitled to more support under state and county guidelines. It's a tradeoff in headaches and hassles, to be sure. More paperwork. More assessments. More time juggling calls and appointments. But the results allow me to be home and get her the support she needs. I even get time to myself (very occasionally) during these in-home (now online) therapy sessions. She was never going to get any personally tailored music therapy in public school, much less two to three times a week. She would have continued hating math every day. Instead she brings me math questions and we enjoy solving them together.

In our case, we were already video conferencing with friends and partially educating online, so COVID-19 has been easier to adapt to in terms of what our homeschooling set-up looks like. Please note that I said easier, not easy. Being physically apart from peers and friends is hard, full stop. However, depending on the challenges faced by each family, isolation is not likely to be a new struggle for those with disabilities. We have been struggling to cope with lack of inclusion and lack of access to public events for years. My child's learning environment and many of her therapy-based relationships are already tailored to a one-to-one or small group approach. More classes are now being taught online since the virus hit, which gives my daughter surprisingly more access to social interaction and learning opportunities than before.

PARTING WORDS

I'd like to give a few words of encouragement to those who are newly joining the homeschool community.

For many of us, following the restrictions to stop the spread of COVID-19 throws our work/family life balance wildly off course. It takes a lot to figure out how to effectively redistribute our personal time and energy. That's really hard to manage with children who used to be at school now clamoring for direction and suddenly always underfoot. Forcing a child who has been unexpectedly uprooted from the routine of public school into a hastily altered online version of public school from home doesn't usually go well. That's "crisis schooling," not "homeschooling." Trying to recreate public school at home even without going online is also impossible and exhausting. Grades and assignments under these circumstances will not necessarily reflect what your child is capable of attaining in life. If you hold on, it's like a snowball rolling downhill. It will take you down with it. De-schooling is your access to let it go.

In their panic to retain all public-school-based standards and expectations, care providers lost in crisis schooling often miss (or attempt to skip) "Deschooling." But this preparatory phase is necessary before homeschooling can effectively begin. To deschool, care providers and kids must learn to let go of what schooling looks like. There are no attempts at formal schooling during this time. This practice gives everyone a chance to just stop, to see how and when they individually learn best, and at what pace. The general rule of thumb is that children need one month of de-schooling per year of public school attended, although some will need more and some less. Parents also need this time to adjust their own ingrained concept of what "school" looks like. Check with your state homeschooling liaison and local advocacy groups to determine the minimum yearly state testing and reporting requirements (since school districts sometimes de-mand more than they are legally required to receive), and to see if there is a type of acceptable test that best fits your kid's testing style. If academic performance testing is required in your state only once every twelve months, then you really may have more time both to begin with deschooling and to let your child learn at the pace that works best for them. You will then have a chance to step back and evaluate your own capacity for providing educa-tion. Figuring this out means developing new life skills for everyone. It's good to know that once you find your family's new rhythms, homeschool-ing one or two children that you already know well takes far, far fewer hours per day than teaching twenty kids in a classroom. Learning can happen on a set schedule or on weekends—whatever works for your family. Over time, more independent learning and outside support may become available. De-schooling means working smarter, not harder, and it goes by faster than you think.

My biggest wish for all of you is for more patience as you transition to homeschooling. It can make such a difference to let go of what you've im-agined it *should* look like, and just support your kid. Be with your kids on their own terms, if they will let you. Play Minecraft with them or watch their favorite show with them even for just a few minutes a day if that's what it takes. The break may give both of you more room for the different ways your family members each cope with such a life-altering transition. Kids learn all the time despite periods of resistance and upset. This is a transitional space. The old has to be let go of in order to create the new. It's okay to feel overwhelmed. Just recall that snowball analogy and then do your best to let go and trust the process.

For an adult to learn a new language, they say it helps to have a child's mind. Children learn through play and through open-ended curiosity. If at all possible, try to let yourself be open to being playful and curious with your kids instead of judgmental and fearful about their education. If you are trying to work from home and they are not doing their schoolwork, that might (gasp) have to be okay at the beginning. Because trying to force your kid to do something they cannot currently handle is never going to work. When my kid stopped public school I panicked that she would never learn anything and I would fail her. Instead, with time and patience, her natural curiosity and love of learning returned. Eventually.

I hope you all take the necessary deschooling step before attempting this completely new arrangement. Deschooling allows for the critical transition from one form of schooling to another, allows for some grace and breathing room, and leads to a more workable future.

Take the long view. Remember what you have seen your child achieve when you were sure they were never going to make that first step or say that first word. Both you and your kids have a chance to trust their own internal processes more when given room to explore those processes. Deschooling does that.

Development is driven internally. If your kid is passionate about becoming an engineer, they are going to figure out the math and science regardless of how many assignments get missed. Or perhaps all they want to do right now is play the trumpet. You may have a classical musician blooming and you have a front row seat. Maybe they can't do anything like that, but there is something new that has been waiting to surface. Parents of disabled children are deeply aware of the hindrances and gifts of developmental challenges. If you homeschool, you may get to provide space and encouragement to your child on their terms.

I believe in you and your kids. I believe in how deeply committed and resourceful you all are when it comes to achieving an education under difficult circumstances. Take it one moment at a time. That's all we really have, right?

---

[1] Regina Merchant, "Relief is Everything: The Homeschooling Journey of a Special Needs Family," *SEA Homeschoolers*, October 19, 2018, https://seahomeschoolers.com/home-school_special_needs.

7

KELLEY CHRISTIE

Kelley and her husband Taylor have two children, ages five and eight, who they have been home educating since 2018. Kelley has a bachelor's degree in Finance from Indiana University. She is a former high school math teacher at both a boarding school and a public school, and she is a private math teacher for homeschool students. Kelley also wrote curriculum for an alternative high school in Vermont. She is an outdoor enthusiast, and founder of the "Wild Toes" outdoor education program (www.wildtoes.com). She and her family live in the Boston, Massachusetts area with their rescue dog, Rocka, and their two guinea pigs.

ABOUT OUR FAMILY

On a typical day, just as the sun rises, you'll find my eight-year-old daughter and me returning from walking our dog. When we get home, my five-year-old daughter is usually just waking up, in time for us all to have breakfast together. Then it's time for my husband to leave for work—he runs his own HVAC company. Pretty quickly after breakfast the day unfolds and chores are waiting. Before we allow the day to steal the precious calm, we curl up for our morning reading time. Sometimes we read a stack of picture books, and sometimes a novel. Our two guinea pigs might love read-aloud time as much as we do, as they are often curled up in the girls' laps or running around on the floor. Read-aloud time is my favorite, most treasured time and I will not allow it to be pushed aside by the mounting to-do list.

I never knew I would be a homeschooling parent. It came about rather organically. I didn't send my kids to preschool—I never found a preschool that allowed the unrestricted outdoor free time I felt was vital for self-discovery, learning, and happiness. Plus, I love learning, and even more so, love learning alongside my children. It just felt natural to keep them with me during those fundamental years of birth to age five.

We transplanted to Massachusetts from Vermont in 2016 and were shocked by the difference in outdoor play for children in our new town. The playgrounds and trails around us were vacant. Where were all the kids? An overwhelming number of kids were in some form of childcare, often associated with "enrichment opportunities," i.e., ballet, soccer, Russian School of Math, violin lessons, preschool, etc. All of these activities are wonderful learning opportunities, but when piled one on top of another, they eliminate play time/free time, which is devastating for healthy childhood development. This is a core value in our family—the belief that every child has a right to play, and also the space to be bored, and therefore, have the opportunity to be creative. This value is at the root of our homeschooling.

Once my oldest daughter reached school age in 2017, we began the traditional route of public schooling. I grew up going to public schools and loved my school experience. So it was natural for me to choose that route, never realizing we had other schooling options. My daughter loved school in the beginning, thriving with a wonderful teacher, and she was still home by 11:30 am to enjoy plenty of unrestricted outdoor play time. There were issues that frustrated all of us, from five-minute snack times and very restrictive recess activities to limited access to books. But these grievances were bearable in the quantities of 2.5 hours per day. Once first grade began, and occupied her day from 8:00 am to 4:30 pm, the issues became heavy and intolerable. I noticed my daughter's love of learning beginning to be smothered by the educational system. My daughter came home the first week of school asking to be homeschooled. I was terrified at the prospect. How do I homeschool? What are the regulations? How do I know what to teach? How do I do this all within the legal guidelines? Will my daughter be happy? I pushed back and tried to help her continue at school, but she cried every day begging to stay home. Finally, I tackled my own fear, discovered the ease of submitting my educational plan, as required in Massachusetts, and withdrew my daughter within the first month of her first grade year.

Those first few weeks homeschooling, in hindsight, were spent with me frantically trying to recreate school at home. I didn't know any better. We sat at the kitchen table, for too many hours, doing too many worksheets. I was driven by fear. Once I let go and recognized my daughter has an innate and insatiable desire to learn, we finally found our rhythm.

We are currently finishing up our second year of homeschooling and I'm not sure I can classify our homeschooling into any one style. It is an eclectic mix, and our homeschool looks different depending on the day of the week. Our homeschooling looks like this: We joined a small, informal homeschool co-op consisting of about eight families; we enjoy an abundance of read-aloud time; we play outside for three to five hours per day (sometimes upwards of ten hours on days when we just can't escape the charismatic pull of sun and nature); and I follow the lead of my kids' interests, incorporating reading, math, science, and history into those contexts. More often than not though, my kids tend to create their own learning experiences without me prompting the topic, the activity, or the result. The intrinsic motivation, the meaningful topics, and the creative output are driven by their own desires to learn.

WHAT I LOVE ABOUT HOMESCHOOLING

Flexibility!

I love the flexibility to visit nearly empty museums in the middle of the week. I love the flexibility to read for two hours and incorporate history, before we've even had breakfast. I love the flexibility that allows my children to read any book they choose, and to dive into the book deeper via any relevant meaningful method. I love the flexibility to do meaningful math rather than just worksheets. I love the flexibility to spend any amount of time on any topic we choose rather than feel rushed to finish, or worse, to experience the drudgery of the never-ending irrelevant topics. I love the flexibility to read outside under the calls of the birds and the shade of the maple trees. I love the flexibility to build strong relationships with children of all different ages and backgrounds, since there's time for deep meaningful play and conversations.

Love of Learning

I love watching my kids love learning. My youngest daughter just turned five and is learning to read on her own. I have never prompted or asked her to learn her letters. Quite the opposite, she has asked me what letters look like and how to spell words. After we read as a family for an hour, she uses her reading lamp to get just a few extra minutes of reading time in on her own before she sleeps.

HOMESCHOOLING CHALLENGES

As the mother doing 100% of the homeschooling, I often find myself feeling self-imposed pressure to make sure I'm doing everything right. There are days when I think, "Yes, we are rocking this thing, we're happy and everyone's engaged!" There are also days when I think "Oh my gosh, what are we doing? The kids are listless, I don't feel prepared, and all we've done is eat!" I think it's natural for us parents to question our effectiveness. I also realize that not every day is going to be perfect, no matter what path we choose.

Each year we evaluate our homeschool time: Did we accomplish our goals? Is homeschooling still working for all family members? The answer to both questions so far has always been yes. Our foundational homeschooling goal is to ignite and fuel the love of learning. As long as my kids love learning and we the parents also feel the thirst to learn, then we're meeting our goals.

PARTING WORDS

Homeschooling looks different for every family, which is what makes it such an amazing educational opportunity. Families are able to tailor their educational path to fit the needs of not just the kids, but all family members. I feel so fortunate that we have this option to educate our own children. It allows us the time to instill our family values on a daily basis. It allows us the time to help guide our kids as they navigate our complex social world and the abundance of life to be learned, in meaningful ways that make sense to our family. Through the flexibility and love of learning made possible by homeschooling, we can help our kids fuel that educational fire inside for a lifelong journey of learning.

8

MARY JO TATE

Mary Jo homeschooled her four sons for twenty-three years. She has a B.A. in English and philosophy from the University of Mississippi and an M.A. in American Literature from the University of South Carolina. She is an international book editor and the author of Flourish: Balance for Homeschool Moms *and* Critical Companion to F. Scott Fitzgerald. *A lifelong bibliophile, she teaches online literature classes to help high schoolers and adults understand, appreciate, and love great books (www.MaryJoTate.com). Mary Jo enjoys speaking at education, writing, and business conferences, and she has a heart to help, encourage, and inspire other moms. You can connect with her at www.FlourishAtHome.com.*

ABOUT OUR FAMILY

I had always planned to be at home with my children, so when I heard about homeschooling, it made perfect sense. Why would I suddenly send them off to spend every weekday with someone else when they turned five? Everyone has a different path, but for me, homeschooling began as a logical continuation of my role as a stay-at-home mom. I have just completed my twenty-third and final year of homeschooling my four sons

55

from kindergarten through twelfth grade, and we wouldn't trade that experience for anything.

I've always loved reading, so Charlotte Mason's emphasis on living books and the classical approach's emphasis on joining the great conversation of classic literature appealed to me. Our home has always been filled with books, and "Let's go look it up" was my answer to my sons' questions about almost any topic.

While great literature has always been the centerpiece of our homeschool, the way we approached our studies changed over the years. I was very intense and hands-on with my firstborn, and my determination to do everything exactly right made me much too uptight. I still recall my frustration over trying to stage the perfect photo op for our reading of *Caps for Sale*, but the stack of caps wouldn't stay on my son's head. And you know what? It didn't matter. Fortunately, I eventually loosened up—*a lot*—and learned to let go of my unrealistic, perfectionistic expectations.

As I began to include the younger boys in our homeschool activities, I had to figure out how to handle more than one student. We did lots of reading aloud, independent reading, narrating, and discussing what they were learning. I taught them together whenever possible—especially for subjects like history, literature, and science—and focused our one-on-one time on skills like math and phonics. We participated in field trips and other activities with our local homeschool support group, which provided a community for parents and students alike.

Then our world fell apart. My husband left to live with another woman when our sons were nine, six, four, and six months old. I was committed to remaining at home and continuing to homeschool my children, but I had no idea how I could make it happen. But God provided for us in many ways, including help from my parents, assistance from our church, and building up my freelance editing business.

As I worked to grow my business, manage the home on my own, and establish a new family identity, I realized that our homeschooling would need to change as well. One year a dear friend from church included my boys in her family's weekly unit study. Another year, we participated in a unit-study co-op. Eventually we joined a classical Christian homeschool co-op for Friday classes for nine years, and my youngest son took some of his high school classes at a private school where I taught for four years. As I learned, there's no One Right Way to homeschool. The right way is what works for you and your family.

WHAT I LOVE ABOUT HOMESCHOOLING

I'm an ardent advocate for homeschooling because the benefits are nearly endless. Homeschooling allows your family to share all of life together in the real world rather than being separated into age-segregated classrooms. It's a wonderful way to strengthen parent-child bonds and sibling relationships. My sons—now ages twenty-eight, twenty-five, twenty-three, and nineteen—are still great friends who frequently consult one another and enjoy spending time together.

Students can learn at their own pace. For example, most of my boys were advanced in English and a bit behind in math, and that was just fine. They didn't have to fit every subject into a single-grade box. They had time to pursue their own interests, and they developed independent learning skills and habits of responsibility that later helped them in college and jobs.

Homeschooling doesn't have to look like a classroom. Children can learn while gathered around the dining-room table or snuggled up together on the sofa reading aloud. They can learn at home, on a field trip, at the library, or in the car. They can even learn while perched on top of the swing set with a book, as one of my boys preferred to do at age ten. One of my favorite memories is reading *The Swiss Family Robinson* aloud under a shady tree in our front yard. I was delighted when the mail carrier asked the thirteen-year-old, "Shouldn't you be in school today?" and he replied, "We're doing school right now."

All of life is an opportunity for learning. You'll probably use at least some curriculum, but there's also a whole world outside the textbooks.

Here are just a few of the ways my children learned that don't necessarily look like "school": planting a sunflower garden and running inside for a beloved field guide to identify an interesting insect, going on a mission trip to Peru, discovering a new drawing technique by trial and error, attending business conferences with me, asking theological questions out of the blue, making bread, acting out stories and history lessons with stuffed animals or Playmobil figures, and comparison shopping at the grocery store.

Education isn't about memorizing and regurgitating facts. It's about understanding, appreciating, and loving many worthy things. Charlotte Mason explains it well: "The question is not,—how much does the youth know? when he has finished his education—but how much does he care? and about how many orders of things does he care? In fact, how large is the room in which he finds his feet set? and, therefore, how full is the life he has before him?"[1]

Homeschooling is flexible. You can customize your approach, content, and schedule to suit *your* unique family and life. And the details may change every year, depending on the age and abilities of your students, as well as everything else going on in your life, such as a new baby, illness, job loss, or moving.

HOMESCHOOLING CHALLENGES

Nineteen of my twenty-three years of homeschooling happened while I was a single mom. It's not the life I dreamed of, but it was still a good life, and God was faithful.

I've already mentioned some of the ways we dealt with single-parent homeschooling by participating in co-ops and classes, but we also learned many other strategies that may help any family facing challenges. As soon as my sons became competent readers, I encouraged independent learning. When they were older, I provided a weekly assignment sheet each Monday and was available to answer questions and discuss what they were studying.

They all studied the same period of history, and the older boys read easy books aloud to the younger boys as well as reading books at their own levels.

(Bonus tip: A well-written children's book is one of the best introductions to any subject, so older students learn even when they read to younger siblings.) Other ways to delegate or outsource part of the teaching include tutors, audiobooks, video courses, software, and online classes.

Challenges aren't limited to homeschooling itself. Balancing studies with parents' jobs, home businesses, and other responsibilities can be tough. Life is a marathon, not a sprint, so it's important to find a pace you can maintain for the long haul. Constantly operating in overdrive is a surefire recipe for burnout. If you're suddenly adding homeschooling to an already-busy life, you have to find some things to eliminate in order to make space and time for it. Remember: Opportunity doesn't equal obligation; it's okay to say no even to good things in order to say yes to the best things.

If something can't be eliminated, often it can be delegated. Helping with housework, laundry, cooking, and other chores teaches children responsibility and makes them feel like they're contributing to the family in a meaningful way. Depending on your budget, many household and business tasks can be outsourced so that you can focus on what's most important.

Were our homeschooling years easy? Definitely not. But they strengthened our family, brought lots of joy, and helped my sons to become responsible adults. I would do it all over again in a heartbeat.

PARTING WORDS

My most important advice for homeschoolers—whether brand-new or experienced—is this: Find peace in the space between the ideal and reality. The ideal is what you would do and have if you could do and have anything you want without any of the complications of ordinary life. The reality is the facts of your everyday life. What will you do in the middle?

There will never be a perfect time or place for homeschooling. Life will always present challenges, whether big or small. Instead of being disappointed and paralyzed by what you can't do, focus on what you can do and how you and your family can best use each day's opportunities.

Remember that homeschooling is not just about academics; it's also about building character and nurturing relationships. When my youngest son was four, he announced, "I want to do school." When I asked what kind of schoolwork he wanted to do, he replied, "I want to do the kind of school where the whole family sits down together and draws or reads a story. That's the kind of school I like."

There's a lot of wisdom in that. Whatever homeschooling approach you choose, be sure to make room in your life for the whole family sitting down and learning together.

---

[1] Charlotte Mason, *School Education: Developing a Curriculum* (Tyndale House, 1989), 170–171.

9

MATTHEW PARKS

Matthew and his wife Bonnie have five children ages three to twelve, and decided to homeschool when their oldest was around two years old. Matthew graduated from BYU in 2007 with a bachelor's in Computer Science. He's an ice cream passionista and proud recipient of the Ben & Jerry's Golden Scoop award. Matthew is a co-founder of About Connection (www.aboutconnection.com), a start-up focused on strengthening relationships. Currently he resides near Richmond, Virginia.

ABOUT OUR FAMILY

In November, 2018 we said goodbye to our home in Utah and began traveling from one state to another, staying in vacation rentals along the south and east coasts of the U.S. After ten months we settled in the Richmond, Virginia area. We loved the adventure, the experiences, and the craziness of this unique lifestyle, even though it wasn't the extended vacation I kind of hoped it would be. After all, we were still parents and homeschoolers!

We decided to homeschool when our first child, now almost thirteen years old, was about three. Thankfully, this means our ten-month long dramatic change in lifestyle didn't include taking on homeschooling for the first time.

You might say, "Wow, ten whole years of experience, they probably have it all figured out by now," . . . and we would laugh. Early on we'd find *this* curriculum or *that* method and think "Yes! We've got it! We have everything in place for all our children for their entire education!" We were a little naive. As it turns out, the education of our children is as much a process for us as it is for them. That said, there are a few principles we've learned along the way to aid us in our approach.

Have you ever focused so much on a process that you missed the purpose? Looking back, I think we experienced some of this until we pondered one fundamental question: What do we want our kids to have when they leave our home? For us, it comes down to five core areas of development: character, relationships, mission/purpose, scholarship, and stewardship.

Education means much more to us now than just *school*; education is a part of *everything* we are and do.

Recently for *Dad Class*, two of my daughters and I have been learning to crochet. One daughter has picked it up with ease while the other has struggled, so this morning while we worked, we chatted about talents and grit. They may or may not crochet again, their small scarves probably won't endure, and I doubt they'll remember our discussion, but repeated experiences like this influence our relationships and our family culture.

Some of our most impactful education comes from the culture we experience. As a result, my wife and I have become proactively cautious about the media our children consume. What messages does it send about ethics and character? About God? About kindness and boundaries? About violence? About sex? And on and on. No, we're not trying to raise our kids in a bubble, oblivious to the harsh realities of life. Rather, we wish to raise them in a greenhouse where they can develop strong roots and be prepared to face those harsh realities with valor.[1]

So on one hand, we try to be aware and intentional about the cultural messages they receive—we value hard work, so we give them a good bit of work to do; we value scholarship, so we teach them a good bit of academics; we value their relationship with God, so we have daily scripture study and weekly religious observances. On the other hand, we believe everything they do *counts*—it's all part of their education. Playing board games? Part of their education. Riding bikes around the neighborhood, with or without friends? Part of their education. Reading a book for fun? Part of their education.

We no longer expect one program, curriculum, or method to serve even one of our children for their entire education, nor do we want it to. Instead, we ponder, pray, and focus on what each child needs, then do our best to make available the resources they need for their next step.

WHAT I LOVE ABOUT HOMESCHOOLING

You mean besides sleeping in? Or not having to prep lunches every night and make sure homework is in order? Or not having to revolve every morning around getting the kids to their bus or carpool on time? How about not stressing about upcoming tests? And not getting half-way to school and my child realizing a book got left home or suddenly remembering a huge project due the next day?

I don't know how other parents manage it, day in and day out. It's a monumental pain in the middle ages of life! I suppose, however, that these aren't reasons why I love homeschool, but why I wouldn't love traditional school.

Homeschooling has a lot of benefits, like beating crowds on mid-week field trips, having a flexible time schedule to do something spontaneous, or having freedom to time a family vacation when we wish. While I love these benefits, what I love most about homeschooling comes down to three main ideas: time, choice, and customization.

Time

"Enjoy them while they're young, they grow up so fast!" How many times have I rolled my eyes at this comment? Many. Very many! And yet I believe that time with family is *so* important—not just quality time, but *quantity* time. Most of the values and priorities kids develop are learned from the places and people with whom they spend the most *amount* of time.

In his book *How Will You Measure Your Life?*, the late Harvard professor, Clayton Christensen compared raising children today with the story of Theseus' ship. The Athenians promised to preserve Theseus' ship and did so, replacing each board when it rotted, each line as it wore out. There came a point at which every single piece had been completely replaced and the philosophical question became: Is it still Theseus' ship?

Between school, jobs, day care, and myriad extra-curricular activities, it seems *hard* for parents to get a lot of *quantity* time with their children!

Christensen explained:

> *I want to turn [Theseus' ship] into a similar philosophical question for you: If your children gain their priorities and values from other people . . . whose children are they?*
>
> *Yes, they are still your children—but you see what I am getting at. . . . The point is that even if you're doing it with the best of intentions, if you find yourself heading down a path of outsourcing more and more of your role as a parent, you will lose more and more of the precious opportunities to help your kids develop their values—which may be the most important capability of all.[2]*

This is *not* intended as a guilt trip. (I believe the majority of parents, ourselves included, are doing the best we can by our kids, and the shame we often feel as parents rarely if ever does any good!) Rather, I'm expressing how homeschooling gives us *a lot* more time with our children, for which I'm grateful. If this was the only benefit of homeschooling, it would be worth doing just for this.

Choice

Mom knows best, or so the saying goes. But frankly, mom doesn't always know best, and dad either. We're doing the best we can, but sometimes we feel like Oscar the Grouch could do a better job! However, while we may not "know best" in every given moment, we do get to *choose* how we raise our children.

Child psychologist Dr. Gary Thompson often says, "Parents are and always will be the resident experts of their own children."[3] Families are the fundamental unit of society. Parents are uniquely entitled to heavenly guidance with regard to the rearing and protection of their children. This includes their education.

I'm grateful to live in a country and a state where we are free to homeschool. Even though my wife handles most of the day-to-day efforts, I have a good sense of what my children are doing and learning. Our children's education is our responsibility as parents, no one else's, and we claim it.

Customization

What is the purpose of education? I love this question. Left alone, it's dealing in the abstract, but it becomes immediately concrete when we add an individual name: "What is the purpose of education for <child's name>?" Each of our children have unique personalities and interests, hopes and fears, dreams and talents. What gives one a sense of purpose in life may not be the same for another. As such, the purpose of education of one child will be significantly different than that of another, unique to his or her individuality.

I love how homeschooling gives us the freedom to tailor each child's education to what they need in order to grow. This coming year, three of our children will be part of a co-op together, each for different reasons. Meanwhile, our oldest is developing her own education plan (with our guidance) while our youngest is insisting she will not be potty-trained! Sigh.

Another customization is that we don't worry about the standards or time tables traditional schooling tries to enforce. The question, "Are they behind?" has little meaning to us. Behind what? Regardless of how much professional and psychological expertise contributes to educational standards, no one-size-fits-all age-based rubric can meet the needs of the wide variety of children it's meant to serve. So, "behind?" In our view, that doesn't hold weight.

Do I mean we don't care about our children's scholarship? Of course not! We care immensely. But *enough* with the idea that a child should have certain abilities by a certain age! Children develop differently. Our six-year-old has been slower at learning to read than his sisters. Are we worried? Not at all; we're here for him and fully confident he'll learn when he's ready.

Requiring learning on a quixotic schedule may achieve a skill by a certain time, but inspiration and creativity are often its casualties. We're more interested in seeing our children read a book when they're thirty-six years old than when they're six years old.

HOMESCHOOLING CHALLENGES

Anticipating the birth of our fifth child, we decided I would run our homeschool for two weeks after the baby was born. I'd like to say I made it through the two weeks; I'd like to say I lasted an entire day! I'm not sure I made it two hours before I came back to our bedroom completely discombobulated, having failed to accomplish even the first thing on the school list. My respect for my wife's skills and endurance, though generally high, were formally enthroned that day! I'd never resonated with the phrase "herding cats" so keenly.

So my wife takes on most of the day-to-day, never-ending, over-stimulating task of our children's schooling. My gratitude is difficult to put into words!

As the parent with less direct involvement in regular instruction, I don't know that my challenges are unique to homeschoolers. It's uncomfortable to share this in so public a way, but the hardest things for me to deal with are feelings of shame—feeling like I'll never be the dad my kids deserve.

It's not a natural impulse for me to proactively engage with my kids. I have to deliberately make time for it and choose it. I praise the idea of spending lots of time with my children and I know the benefits, but actually living it is hard for me.

My preference instead is to throw myself completely into one project or another. I've often thought, "Great, do it, and involve a child!" But the patience required to help my children participate in my projects challenges me to the utmost. I'm so focused on accomplishing the task that it's hard to remember the greater priority: shared experience and learning.

Currently I have three daily *Dad Classes*, one with my oldest, one with my son, and one with our two middle daughters. Each involves a task that I find pleasant but that isn't so important to me that it overcomes the priority of my experience with my children. I'm also involved in our family's *Grammy-School Book Club* and often read a book to/with the family. While it's a meager portion of the formal schooling, it's one of the best arrangements we've found so far to promote my regular involvement.

Yes, we claim the responsibility for our children's education, but that doesn't mean we find it comfortable. It's challenging, and doubts like, "Is what we're doing actually making a difference?" and "Why do we even try?" love to creep in. Because sometimes, neither of us feels like it. Some days it feels easier to give up and let the kids do whatever the heck they want.

Emotions flow, tears fall, apologies are made when needed, and some days are simply a wash. On the good days, though, we can look at those bad days and realize that these, too, *count* as part of their education. It would be impossible to exemplify grit if we only had, or somehow only let our kids see, the good days.

PARTING WORDS

I leave you with two thoughts, one of influence and another of purpose.

Influence

Homeschooling or not, parents' attitudes about education will hold more long-term influence on their children's education than any efforts they make to educate them.

I whole-heartedly agree with sex therapist David Schnarch, Ph.D., when he says: "Kids always map out their parents' attitudes about sex—including when parents say nothing about it."[4] This principle holds true for parents' attitudes on just about everything.

I hope our children feel and believe deep down that our home is a safe place to make mistakes, to be emotional, or to have a hard time. When a child of mine makes a poor choice with significant consequences, which I'm sure will happen, I hope that child never thinks "Oh no, my dad's going to kill me!" Rather, I hope my child thinks "Oh no, I need my dad!" They intuitively know my character—I know I have work to do here—and they're more likely to mirror the character of their parents than of anyone else, sometimes to our chagrin!

So if you want your child to love reading, inspire a love of reading by learning to love reading yourself. If you want your child to cherish honesty and goodness, learn to cherish honesty and goodness yourself. If you want your child to love him/herself and be forgiving, then love yourself and be forgiving. "Be the change that you wish to see in the world."

Purpose

In his book *Teacher and Child,* Dr. Haim G. Ginott described witnessing many atrocities instigated by intelligent and knowledgeable people. He said as a result of this, "I am suspicious of education. . . . My request is: Help your students become human. Your efforts must never produce learned monsters, skilled psychopaths, or educated Eichmanns. Reading, writing, and arithmetic are only important if they serve to make our own children more humane."[5]

Education is bigger than any school. Homeschooling is a term we use when parents take on the academic learning of their children themselves, but home education is a part of every child's life no matter where or what they may call *home.* This is why the family is and always will be the fundamental unit of society. So I invite you to ponder the question: What is the purpose of education for your child?

―――――――――

[1] Marisa Boonstra, "I'm Not Raising My Kids in a Bubble, I'm Raising Them in a Green-house," *Her View From Home: Stories From the Heart of Every Home.* Accessed June 20, 2020 at http://www.herviewfromhome.com/kids-greenhouse. Permission to use granted by Marisa Boonstra.

[2] Clayton M. Christensen, *How Will You Measure Your Life?* (HarperCollins, 2012), 138-139.

[3] Gary Thompson. (March 26, 2020). [Facebook update retrieved from

https://www.facebook.com/DrGary.Thompson.] Used with permission.

[4] David Schnarch, *Crucible® Institute Sexual Desire & Interpersonal Neurobiology Self-Education Course,* Lesson 19.

[5] Haim G. Ginott, *Teacher & Child: A Book for Parents and Teachers* (Avon Books, 1972), 245.

10

MELISSA CALAPP

Melissa is a homeschool graduate, and has spent the last twenty-two years homeschooling her own children. She has worked for the last eleven years for a charter school, guiding, walking with, and supporting thirty-nine other families as they have navigated home-based learning in all its varieties. She has an associate degree in early childhood education, a bachelor's degree in psychology, and teaching credentials in K-8 multi-subject, high school English and high school history. She is the author of Homeschool Adventures: Learning Through the Power of Field Trips. *You can follow her on Instagram at livelearnworkathome.*

ABOUT OUR FAMILY

In the mid-90s, by the second month of my sophomore year, I had had enough of the brick and mortar school and asked my mom to sign me up for a new type of school, known as a home-based charter school. I'd still have to meet requirements but could do it in whatever way I chose, and I'd have a teacher who met with my mom once a month to help guide me through and get me supplies. Within three months, I had decided I'd be homeschooling my children someday. At sixteen, I began studying educational philosophy, and especially various methods of homeschooling. I married young and my husband loved the idea of homeschooling, so when baby number one came along, I considered us a homeschooling family and deepened my study of education. That baby is now twenty-two, and he and my twenty-year-old daughter are in college. I still have a senior, sophomore, eighth-grader, fifth-grader and kindergartener. Yes, that's seven, and they have all been homeschooled all the way through.

I am rather eclectic in my homeschooling methods. Most days we do a morning time that we call "together-school." All of the school-age children are encouraged to participate. The younger ones are often in and out but mostly on my lap. For some periods, the oldest school-age child has been too busy to participate. During our together-school I'm usually in a rocking chair with my basket of supplies next to me and the kids are sprawled on the couch, chairs, or floor. What we do changes depending on the day and may last from twenty minutes to two hours. We read and discuss fiction, non-fiction, and poetry. We study artists, musicians, or a musical time period. We learn Latin and Greek root words, Spanish, and Sign Language. Sometimes I review flashcards on geography, spelling rules, artists, and various other subjects. Sometimes I set up stations around the room for the kids to do while I read. Sometimes I offer them a challenge to do while I read, sometimes they do their own quiet projects, and occasionally, but very rarely, they just sit quietly while I read. What we do during together-school changes quite a bit from day to day—and occasionally we skip it altogether.

After we are done working together, the older kids go to do their independent work and I help the younger ones. This work can and often does include online live classes, online programs, workbooks, lots of reading, some videos, and their own research and activities. In typical years it includes one to six live in-person weekly classes. My older children have taken some community college classes while in high school as well. Did I mention we're pretty eclectic? Before each semester I look at how each child is doing, and think about any areas they may need to focus on. I get their input and we choose curriculum and methods that seem like a good fit for each of the core areas, and then we add in other studies that may be of particular interest or need to that child. Sometimes I'll tell the kids what classes are available in the community during times that work for our family and ask them what they would like to take. This has included a lot of musical theater, piano, computer lab courses, horseback riding, woodshop, dance, and dozens of other things. I often give preference to courses that several of my children can take at the same time, or locations that offer multiple courses concurrently for different ages. I have taught high school classes at our house once a week for the last two years to two of mine plus seven other students. I used our local standards and studied the needs of these nine students, and then designed and taught three courses that I felt would stretch them. While my house was filled with teenagers, another mom took two of my younger children to attend classes by other parents at a different location. My youngest who was three and then four learned to play quietly or just be held while I taught, with the promise that she could visit with all the teens on their breaks.

We have also been part of a homeschool field trip group for the last six years. We have gone nearly every Thursday, meeting up with between five and fourteen other families. We have toured wastewater treatment centers, nature preserves, factories, museums, historic homes, and hundreds of other places. I often try to pre-teach something a day or two before the trip and then provide a follow-up activity to help the children retain information or put the places in context. You can find more about how I do this in my book *Homeschool Adventures: The Power of Learning Through Field Trips*.

WHAT I LOVE ABOUT HOMESCHOOLING

I love the ability to customize what the kids are doing, each to their own preferences. I have some very artistic children and others who love nothing more than to take computers apart. One pursued acting and directing, winning a student film contest with a friend, competing against full site-based high school programs. Another worked with a mentor to learn to take apart and tune pianos. I have children who spend their free time reading and others who only read when needed or required. My children have had so many opportunities that would have been more difficult if a system controlled all their time. By taking charge of their education I have been able to customize plans, lessons, and methods to each child.

I love the relationships that develop through homeschooling. My children are each other's best friends and greatest confidants. Their creativity builds on each other and they have always played together, designing complex games with conflict that must be managed and rules that are carefully made and must be strictly followed. They have gone on to create board games and write stories both together and separately, building on all the creativity they have developed over the years.

I love the opportunities we occasionally have to speed up or slow down depending on current needs. Sometimes I can see a character trait that may cause future problems if not addressed soon, and I can pause or change our schooling to address it. For instance, I like my children to be able to work hard for sustained periods of time by their mid-teens. Partially in order to teach this, we moved to land where there would be more work to do. I began reading them stories of children and teens in pioneer and other times when hard things happened and the characters learned to work together, be creative, and solve real problems. (I often choose our read-aloud novels to particularly emphasize something and create a lot of discussion.) We then decided that Thursday mornings before our field trips would be agriculture days. We'd watch videos of families working on farms and the creative projects they were doing, and then together we would go work on a project around our little farm. We also decided that Saturdays would include four to six hours of chores for the older children and parents. Soon our kids were able to put in a longer workday. I'm proud of the name they are making for themselves in the community as hard workers now. My sixteen-year-old spent the summer putting in eight- to twelve-hour days cleaning carpets with a company who was very happy to have him.

I also love that homeschooling gives us a lot of opportunity for heart-to-heart talks, as I select read-alouds meant to create discussion, and sometimes we are side-tracked and scrap the rest of the morning school to talk about one particular topic. Since we are often together, I can monitor behavior and pull the children aside for discussion or to help me with an activity quickly when distraction is needed.

I love that our homeschooling has become part of our family culture, and it has given us the flexibility we need to create the vision of the family and life we want to create.

HOMESCHOOLING CHALLENGES

When you homeschool and parent for twenty-two years, you are apt to run into a lot of challenges. We have moved twelve times and have lived through the real estate collapse, where we lost our home and moved in with another family. We have squished into a two-bedroom duplex, and now we are in an older home with about an acre and a half of land, and spend many days on remodeling plans and various outside projects.

I have a couple of children with special needs, and have needed to figure out systems for meeting different food needs and environmental needs. I've spent days with children seeing doctors and then recuperating in hospitals. I've sat with a child during their time in a wheelchair and then learning to walk again. I've cried with children over all the emotions of their different situations and various struggles, and I've hugged and kissed them and sometimes just sat for hours holding them. For teens, these sometimes (often) come late into the night, and that's part of it.

But for me the biggest challenge has been one of balance. During my entire adult life I have always worked or been in school. I have been a writer, virtual assistant, appraisal assistant, realtor, and for the last eleven years I have worked as a support teacher for a home-based charter school similar to the one that helped me back when I was in high school. This lets me help others on this homeschooling journey, and I love meeting with families and guiding and helping them find resources, patterns, and new techniques.

It is a state teaching position and thus includes a lot of record keeping for auditors, which I love a bit less. I usually have my students for years and tend to be very invested in how they do, and I have such a desire to do a lot for my students and families. I reevaluate very often how much I can do for others, how many students I can take, how much I need to be available for my own family, and occasionally, I even do things to take care of myself.

My job is mostly from home, but also typically includes meeting with the charter school families weekly to monthly at their homes. I also have monthly staff meetings where I'm gone from three to nine hours. There are online Zoom meetings, trainings, and then the more flexible tasks. I try a variety of ways to manage homeschooling and parenting with the twenty to forty hours of work each week. I often homeschool in the morning and start work at 1 pm, going until bedtime with an evening break for dinner. Sometimes when student portfolios or reports are coming due, we skip together-school and the kids are on their own most of the day, with just periodic check-ins from me to make sure they are staying on track. I use a large chalkboard on the wall and write their individual assignments on it each day. Each child initials each line when done. I learned long ago I still need to spot check the work to make sure it is really done, and done satisfactorily. We call this "board work," and in spring when it is state testing time and I'm at a site proctoring exams all day on top of all the other things for work, my children may go two weeks just doing board work with no read-alouds and no together-school at all. Sometimes I'm up very late working, and then our school may be less than inspiring for a bit. I always feel like I could be doing better at homeschooling during these times, but I know there are phases and I will pick up the other pieces when I can. I also wouldn't give up the times I do have with my children, watching them learn, and building the family culture that we truly want.

PARTING WORDS

I love to be in a part of the world and a period in history where we have so many options as to how we can educate our children. I know this last year has been particularly rough for so many families. I am currently enrolling families who are confused about what school may look like during the next year. I don't have all the answers, but I can tell you that it can look wonderful. Homeschooling can be examined and designed to fit your particular child and family. It can include all the things that you thought were missing and all the pieces you think they will need. There is room to pursue individual passions. And for parents who are new to homeschooling, you can start slow. You can use self-grading online courses or textbooks and YouTube videos. There is no end to the number of resources available. At this stage of our homeschooling history there are many others willing to travel the homeschooling road with you, to help you find the pieces you need to put together a wonderful situation, one that your children can learn in and from.

It may look different than we expected. My senior was going to dual enroll in college, but since all the junior colleges are online now because of COVID-19, do we still want to? I'm not sure. My middle child really wanted to take tech and shop classes at a shared workspace, but we're still not sure if those will be allowed. Another of my kids is very content to stay home, and I'm interested in stretching her by getting her out to meet new people. I'm not sure how all of that will work yet. But at the same time, I'm finding new resources that I didn't know about previously. Maybe a small, live online class for each of them, maybe time to redesign some of our indoor spaces with stations? Hmm, so many possibilities, so much room for creativity. I'm not sure exactly how our homeschool will look next year yet, but I love the process. I also know that no eighteen-year-old, no matter how they are educated, has a complete education, and my kids don't have to know everything before they head to the next phase, whatever that will look like. They'll study a lot more after they leave our little homeschool.

Don't worry about doing it perfectly or doing it all. Worry more about loving them as best you can and intentionally creating days you and they will both love.

11

ALYSON LONG

Alyson and her husband have two teenage sons who they have worldschooled since birth, in more than fifty countries, including the United Kingdom, Australia, Romania, and Vietnam. Alyson is a leading worldschooling authority and is the author of the book The Seven Year Ditch: Seven Years in Travel. *She supports her family through her blog, www.worldtravelfamily.com.*

ABOUT OUR FAMILY

I reluctantly put my elder son in school when he was just four years old. I didn't want to be parted from him and I knew deep down that it was the wrong decision. But, of course, everyone else was doing it so I went with the flow.

It wasn't a great experience, and before he was seven, I'd pulled him out to be homeschooled. He wasn't learning anything, he'd actually gone backwards in many ways, and had encountered bullying and other unpleasantness.

My younger son was just coming up to school age then, so he has never been to school. They are now both older teens doing IGCSEs (International General Certificate of Secondary Education), but their entire school lives until the coronavirus lockdown hit were spent traveling. This is what many call "worldschooling."

My boys have been to more than fifty countries. They've lived in diverse and extreme cultures, experienced ways of life most couldn't imagine, and tested themselves against huge challenges. They've been to Everest Base Camp. They are qualified scuba divers, ski proficiently, and are dedicated conservation volunteers. They also write and create videos for my professional websites. Their childhood experiences have been immense and they know what the world is like first-hand.

As the coronavirus lockdown hit, we found ourselves trapped. It was immediately obvious that staring at the same four walls every day wasn't going to be a great way to end their childhoods, so we signed them up for IGCSEs through an online school. They slotted right in and are enjoying a few hours of lessons each day. It's really interesting how they've been able to do that. Years of missed school are having no effect on their ability to understand the subjects they're now studying. This draws me to the conclusion that the progression and timetable of learning prescribed by a school environment and group learning is not in any way necessary to understand topics at end-of-high-school level.

They see this new learning style as just another interesting life experience and they're happy to try something new.

WHAT I LOVE ABOUT HOMESCHOOLING

Homeschooling has bought us freedom. Physical freedom to do what we want when we want. I've barely spent a day apart from either of my kids, and their dad has been by their sides too. We're a tight-knit group, we get along just great and there are no "teen issues" whatsoever.

Homeschooling has allowed the boys to learn what they want when they want and to follow their interests. They have read more books than most adults. They always read as we travel and they choose the books and truly read for pleasure. They've never had a book forced on them as most of us experience in school and they've had so much more time for reading than school kids.

They developed a passion for ancient history so we packed them off to Egypt and Greece for weeks on end. They learned more on this topic through reading, their own online research and, interestingly, gaming. If you look at the Assassins Creed games, you'll see what I mean. This game recreates Ancient Greece and particularly Delphi, in accurate detail. They've been there, it's great to see this ancient site in a game.

As they got older, they took a few short courses in various topics. Most were free. They dipped into Open University, Outschool, and Minecraft Homeschool, plus a few others. This is the beauty of homeschooling—there are so many resources available at all levels, and the kids are free to choose what interests them and go into their topic in as much depth as they choose. A classroom really is the worst way to get an education, with its total limitation of real-world, real-life experience and opportunity. It cuts kids off from the outside world and from their true interests and passions.

Mostly I love homeschooling because I've been able to spend all my time with my kids.

HOMESCHOOLING CHALLENGES

At this moment, I honestly can't think of any challenges of homeschooling, only benefits. It's been wonderful. The only tricky part is dealing with people who don't get it. Sometimes these people are immediate family. My kids are more important to me than other relatives, so they come first.

For us, it has been expensive. The travel we've done and the places we've taken them have required a huge financial commitment. Travel and education as a product of travel were our priority, so this was never an issue.

Now the online schools they are in are also expensive, but I'm sure you could find cheaper ways.

PARTING WORDS

We never intended for our kids to slot into school later. The plan was for them to be fully educated outside school but home confinement changed our plans. So far it's working out well. We never saw exams as necessary because in my business, they aren't necessary. I'm a self-employed web geek and every skill I use today is self-taught. So we know, for sure, that bits of paper from school aren't necessary for a financially secure and happy future. Of course, that doesn't mean sitting exams because you choose to is a bad idea. Everyone should be free to take the path they choose and anything is possible.

The school way is not the only way.

12

CRISSI ALLEN

Crissi's pride and joy are her two beautiful children, ages twenty-nine and twenty-four, whom she is blessed to have educated for twenty years. Crissi is the founder and director of the co-op HEART Academy (www.heartacademysj.com). She recently started a Facebook group called "HEART Community." She also has businesses in both healthy body and Christian soul coaching (www.crissiallen.com). She received an interdisciplinary degree in Psychology, Sociology, and Anthropology. She currently resides in San Jose, California with her husband, mom, and chihuahua, Evie. Her other pride and joy is her grandson!

ABOUT OUR FAMILY

I received a public school education, so that's what I thought my kids would receive, too. However, God redirected me, and we started homeschooling after two months of kindergarten for my first child—and with a baby to take care of. Homeschooling was convenient for me at that time because I didn't want to drive back and forth to school. It was difficult for the first couple of years. My focus was in the wrong place and I didn't have a deep-down foundation or philosophy of education. Why in the world was

I homeschooling? I started attending statewide homeschooling conventions, and that's when I began to truly understand that homeschooling was a movement of families who wanted to instill good values in their children, give them the best education for their learning style, and prepare them to be a light of love to a dark world. Once I wrote down my reasons, I created my philosophy of education. Eventually, I decided to teach an ABC's of Homeschooling course to help others create a solid foundation as well. If you want to homeschool, you must first write down your reasons for homeschooling. So, why do you want to homeschool your children?

WHAT I LOVE ABOUT HOMESCHOOLING

Oh homeschooling, how do I love thee? Let me count the ways!

To me, first and foremost is the ability to instill in my children the Christian values that are so important to me. I knew that the agendas in public or private schools were not the ones I wanted to subject my children to. Instead, I wanted to teach them to love God with all their heart, soul, mind, and strength. And then, they could love others as themselves. I wanted to pray and read the Bible to them and with them while in our PJs. I wanted their hearts to be soft toward God and not hard towards Him. I wanted to capture their hearts for Jesus.

My second reason for homeschooling is related to time. Homeschooling afforded me the time to skip setting the alarm clock—and not to be rushing out the door in the morning with packed lunches in hand. It gave me the time to be relaxed and present with my children while they were at their best—and not to miss six to eight hours of their "aha" moments every day. We had the time to put family first and take our children with us as my husband traveled to different parts of the country for work. We had the time to create for them the natural rhythm of operating on their own schedule. If our teens needed to sleep in, they could.

Third, tailoring our kids' education individually was vitally important to us. I want the best for them and love them unconditionally. There is a great satisfaction when you teach your own children, and I felt that satisfaction after graduating both of my children from our homeschool. We did not put them on the escalator of cookie-cutter education and busy work, but instead became personally involved with their education. And, oh, the field trips! I loved those times, because I was learning with them! My favorite was our regular visits to the Monterey Bay Aquarium.

If a curriculum didn't work for us, we just set it aside and chose something else. As my children got older, we were able to focus on their passions, because after all, you can only do four or five hours of academics before you're pooped out. Extracurricular activities abounded because we had extra time to do them. My children loved to be involved in musicals and theatrical activities and I went along with them. (In fact, I decided to produce musicals because of them—I produce three musical productions per year, partnering with parents and students.) In addition, life skills were easily added to their repertoire because we lived it, hands-on!

Fourth, we wanted our kids safe and protected until we let go of our hothouse transplants and sent them into the world. The psyches of our children are being damaged by the current public school culture—from unsupervised recess time to books I feel are inappropriate in children's libraries. It's not safe sometimes. I wanted to safeguard their innocence. Bullying is high on the list of reasons why many families start homeschooling. We can't shield our children from everything, but we can help them avoid the difficulties of negative peer influences. Both our children are now young adults and I'm so proud of them as they navigate confidently through their lives.

HOMESCHOOLING CHALLENGES

There will be challenges in your children's lives whether you homeschool, private school, or public school. But I know that if they had been at school, they wouldn't have received the personalized care they received from me, their mom who wants the best for them and will love them, whatever issues fell in front of us. Here are the challenges I faced.

My first challenge happened with my older child. She started to get hives while we did spelling. So what did I do? I looked around and compared her to the other homeschooling kids and forced her to do more spelling. She started to cry, and then I knew something was wrong. She was saying things like, "I feel stupid." We went to a specialized optometrist and found out that she has mild dyslexia. I had to humbly apologize to my child. I almost lost her heart. The solution was to measure her differently than other children her age and take a slower pace with academic work. We started reading great books together as a family because she couldn't read them herself. We worked at capturing her heart again. I'm so glad I discovered her dyslexia sooner than later; homeschooling her helped me do that. To this day, she calls us for advice, even at age twenty-nine. These children think outside the box, and she is currently an influential life-giving entrepreneur, working as the CEO of her own vocal and piano studio.

My second difficulty came through health issues. My younger daughter had headaches for two years. We took her to three or four doctors, not knowing which one was the best for her. Some of the doctors wanted to put her on steroids and we very politely said no. She was only seven and then eight years old. Instead, we started with nutrition and switched to eating only organic foods. I started exclusively using non-toxic products in my home. After going to a chiropractor who specializes in nutrition, subluxations, and emotive kinesiology, we discovered that on top of an allergy to wheat, she was grieving for her friend who had moved away. Homeschooling her was strategic because we were able to adjust the schooling according to how she felt that day. In fact, we didn't do math for one whole year. With these changes, we were able to help her body heal naturally without medication.

Challenges come to make you stronger. I've had my share. Despite the difficulties, I would homeschool all over again!

PARTING WORDS

By far, one of the greatest things about homeschooling is being able to prioritize family relationships. We know our kids better than anyone else does, we love them, and we want the best for them. Because of the time our children spend together, they create strong sibling bonds. It is a privilege to see them socialize with different ages and all get along together. In addition, we are able to volunteer and serve together as a family.

Dive in, the water's fine!

13

MARY PAUL

Mary lives in Georgia with her husband Raymond, one dog, and three neurodiverse kids ages nine, seven, and five. She spends her days homeschooling, gardening, and writing for her blog, www.homeschooling2e.com. Her work discusses the quirks of homeschooling intense kids while simultaneously living with chronic illness. Mary has written articles for Gifted Homeschoolers Forum *and* SEA Homeschoolers, *is published in an academic collection titled* A Press Divided: Newspaper Coverage of the Civil War, *and provides educational materials on the educational website "Teachers Pay Teachers" under the name "Homeschooling2e."*

ABOUT OUR FAMILY

I've always thought you can learn a lot about people by looking at their countertops. The kitchen is the heart of our home. It's where everything goes that doesn't have a place, where active projects sit to dry or finish, and in our case, where schoolwork piles up.

I looked at my countertop tonight and wryly thought it was a pretty accurate snapshot of our lives and our homeschooling. There's a pile of seed packets and garden stuff, a mess of fruit hanging out in the corner, and that one lonely butternut squash waiting for me to do *something* to it.

Over by the table, there are three little jars, each holding bewildered aphids and a baby praying mantis. With a paper towel rubber-banded around the tops, because aphids have a knack for escaping and I do NOT want to find them all over my kitchen!

There's the inevitable pile of bills in the corner, along with the pile of things-that-need-to-be-filed. The boring stuff. In the other corner sits the shrimp tank: a green mass of tangled aquatic plants covered in tiny little red freshwater shrimp just hanging out and breeding like rabbits. Beside them is my daughter's newest fascination: a small tank full of roly-polies, or pill bugs.

In between all of this sits a pile of school stuff. It's the end of the year for us, and I'm immersed in finishing up the kids' school portfolios. Samples of handwriting, math problems, and artwork litter the counter, scattered between my notes and field trip paraphernalia. Judging from our countertops, it's pretty obvious that we're homeschoolers.

Hi, I'm Mary. I'm the lead parent and instructor for our family of three kids and two adults, one dog, and about two hundred shrimp.

All of our kids are some form of Gifted or Twice Exceptional (Gifted plus learning disabilities). This makes homeschooling, well, *interesting* doesn't fully cover the depth of what it's like, but it's a good start. Just to make things more *interesting*, I'm also a chronically ill, disabled individual, and a second-generation homeschooler.

We've been homeschooling for four years now, more if you count the preschool that was really kindergarten level for our oldest. We didn't plan to homeschool. No, that happened accidentally, as a result of the school system. About four years ago, we scheduled an Individualized Education Program (IEP) evaluation for our rising kindergartener, even before he was registered for school. The process didn't go well.

I remember sitting in defeated silence in that drab, slightly dingy conference room, listening to the school psychologist tell us "we want his horizons to widen, not narrow more." Stung, I listened as the rest of the team agreed with the psychologist, telling us that our son wasn't eligible for accommodations that we knew he desperately needed. They decided not to do anything to prepare or support his future teachers, because "he's so smart he'll be able to cope."

The decision to let our son fail, painfully and frustratingly, for multiple months before they would evaluate his case again, was the last straw. We knew that our school district heavily relied on safe rooms and restraints and we didn't want our intense son to end up hurt. That's when we hurtled headlong into the world of homeschooling.

People often ask me what kind of homeschoolers we are. I don't really know how to answer that question. We're somewhere between the full-blown, classical rote-and-repetition academic kind and the completely-child-led unschooling kind. We're eclectic. Secular, eclectic homeschoolers, who pull coursework from a myriad of different resources. We do what works best for each child.

Homeschooling at our house is a rich, immersive, learning-focused experience. Even though the kids are fairly young, they still help pick the subjects they want to learn.

For example, this year my nine-year-old asked if he could blow things up and build robots. Sure! Chemistry and STEM projects went on the list. My seven-year-old requested learning about plants. Great! We studied chlorophyll, photosynthesis, and grew seeds that culminated in a vegetable and flower garden. My five-year-old just wanted to play, so he skipped the worksheets and did puzzles and educational games.

Our normal homeschooling routine now is fairly calm. We did *all the things* for a few years and found that didn't work for our family, so now we deliberately schedule in days at home. A typical week has three fairly intense work days that cover a mix of subjects, a co-op or class day with a lighter work load, and a field trip day. Our state requires 180 instructional days, but we truly school year-round in some form.

WHAT I LOVE ABOUT HOMESCHOOLING

To my children, life filled with hours spent playing pretend or Mario Cart, searching for lightning bugs, riding bikes, and swinging on the tree swing is normal. As an adult with a broader perspective, I cherish their time to be kids. This free time is important to us, partially because of my memories as a homeschooled kid, and partially because our world has become so frantic and stressful. Homeschooling feels like a gift. A gift of safety and security.

Homeschooling is also about depth to us. My kids want to learn "all the things about everything," as my oldest told me once. We're able to dive in as deep as they want and explore subjects without feeling the pressure to move on to the next thing. One year, my oldest was all about carnivorous plants. We learned everything about them, made a field trip to a specialty plant nursery, and even found one type in the pond outside our front door. He did a blue ribbon-winning science project with that knowledge. It was the year of the carnivorous plants!

All of my kids are asynchronous, meaning they are at multiple different grade levels (sometimes wildly different levels) in different subjects. They are advanced in most areas. Homeschooling allows us to tailor their learning to challenge them consistently in a way that Gifted programs in traditional school might not be able to. This is especially true for my Twice Exceptional kids.

My nine-year-old has always struggled with reading. Two years ago, we realized that he had issues with his eyes tracking and focusing. He would decode one word at a time, losing which sentence he was on and jumping to entirely different ones. Nothing made sense and the entire experience was incredibly frustrating for him. Because we're homeschooling, we were able to target his reading needs specifically with therapies and tailored programs that helped him succeed.

If you asked me what my absolute favorite thing about homeschooling is, I would say the flexibility. Homeschooling allows us to follow our own schedule, go traveling when we want, enjoy experiences without crowds, and generally do what works for us.

Flexibility means that we can drop the plans for the day and learn what came up in the moment. For example, ladybugs, on a recent day in our last official week of schooling for this year.

The kids were outside blowing off steam before we started the day. I rambled outside a bit checking plants and making sure none of the kids had a death wish or a deep desire for road rash, as frequently happens around here. I happened to find a ladybug larva scurrying around on one of my plants.

"Kids! Come look what I found!" That's how many of our learning discussions start. They all came running. "A baby ladybug!" I personally think the larvae look like aliens, but my daughter says they're cute. Whatever, child.

"Mom, can we raise it! Please?" My inner homeschooler snickers, like I'm going to say no, right? "We need a food source for them, remember?" They scattered around the yard, hunting for aphids. Once we found a good source of food, then more pressing questions arose. "We need a ladybug house!" they clamored. I hovered over a power drill as they each drilled air holes in lids for their newly found science project. If you've never helped a five-year-old determined to "do it myself!" with a power drill, you haven't experienced a true adrenaline spike!

We were supposed to be finishing up the remaining curriculum for the year. My oldest had vocabulary word lists to write, my middle child had standardized testing to finish, and my youngest had a sight word puzzle I had assigned him. Who cares? Let's do ladybug school instead!

Thankfully, ladybug school happened on a day I was able to handle it. My health is a precarious balance of the right medications, the right phase of the moon, and appeasing whatever random angry nature gods I've offended on that particular day. The flexibility of homeschooling isn't just something I enjoy because it helps my children learn. On some days, that flexibility is the only thing keeping me going.

HOMESCHOOLING CHALLENGES

When we first started homeschooling, I was healthy. Two years ago, I was diagnosed with Rheumatoid Disease (RA), chronic fatigue, chronic migraines, and Occipital Neuralgia, a fancy word for "my joints squish my nerves until they scream." All of a sudden, the person I was disappeared, leaving someone I barely recognized, with major limitations that restrict our homeschooling.

Homeschooling with chronic illness has helped me with my time management and planning. I use the good days to plan ahead and prepare so that on the bad days I don't have to waste my energy. On the really bad days, we're able to take a break so that I can rest and recover.

I certainly wouldn't say that homeschooling with chronic illness is easy. Nothing with chronic illness is easy, to be honest. I know that my illnesses will shorten my lifespan and probably reduce me to an invalid, so I cherish the time I get to spend with my kids through homeschooling. It gives my children more good memories to balance out their memories of my hospitalizations or days parenting from the couch, and I value that highly.

Chronic illness isn't the only challenge our family deals with. All three of the kids have Sensory Processing Disorder (SPD) and anxiety. It manifests differently for each of the kids, but they all have a desperate need to move their bodies. Our schooling involves frequent brain breaks and wiggle breaks.

People often nod in understanding when I say my kids need movement breaks, but it's hard to truly explain what it's like homeschooling with a sensory kid. It's intense, and it's extreme. A tag or an ill-fitting sock can prompt a meltdown, and their bodies are always in motion, desperate for sensory input.

Because of SPD, my nine-year-old's standardized testing took us seven days this year, with sections spread out over multiple days. It's impossible for him to do the Reading Comprehension section in one hour, or even one day. He can complete the work easily, but his brain can't focus on anything after a few minutes besides the pressing need to move his body.

He started fidgeting again and I suppressed a mental sigh. "Do you need a wiggle break?" He jumped up immediately. "Yes!" Off he goes to the mini trampoline that's a fixture in our house and bounced wildly for a few minutes. "Do you feel better now?" I asked. He plopped down in his chair and instantly slid halfway down in the seat. "Yeah." We pressed on, determined to finish this chunk of standardized test before lunch time. That day, I estimate we stopped for a wiggle break every 10 minutes.

Sensory Processing Disorder is a tricky beast. The wrong kind of lights can send my kids into fight-or-flight mode, too many people around them is disorienting, and background noise overwhelms everything else until their brains can't process anything.

Public school would be the equivalent of a permanent panic attack. They would be so focused on survival that learning would become secondary. Homeschooling allows us to avoid that. Home is a safe place, where the lights are calming, the house is visually organized, and the noise level is limited to the hum of fans and talking. If their bodies aren't stressed, then learning is natural and easy.

Their anxiety presents completely different challenges. School refusal happens a lot, where the kids will panic because they think they can't do the work if it's not perfect on the first try. My youngest goes selectively mute when he's frustrated. My older two kids react in a way that looks like defiance, but is still triggered by anxiety.

On our last day of school, my daughter whipped her paper around and scowled. "They're being too noisy!" Both of her brothers were working in different parts of the room, and neither of them were working quietly. "Why don't you take it out to the patio?" I suggested. She did, stalking out with the attitude of an offended teenager. I didn't realize that completing a handwriting sample sheet would demand complete and utter quiet!

A few minutes later she stomped back in, storming because "the wind won't stop blowing my paper!" I suggested she use the desk in the school room away from her brothers. Once finally seated, the real problem quickly became apparent. "I can't do this right! I don't know how to do it! This is TOO HARD!" It took me standing with her and coaching her on the next letter over and over to complete what should have been a simple task. Perfectionism strikes again at the tender age of seven.

My nine-year-old struggles with perfectionism as well. His creative writing suffered for years because he point-blank refused to write anything if it wasn't spelled correctly. He's just now spelling phonetically, a skill his age peers mastered years ago. Building their resilience and helping them practice failing is another life skill that homeschooling allows us to integrate into their education.

All of the challenges our family face are present no matter what type of education we choose for them. That makes my job as their instructor considerably more complicated, but homeschooling is worth it because it reduces their anxiety and stress. Our ability to homeschool allows them to focus on learning instead of on their challenges.

PARTING WORDS

I had this bright idea that I would get the kids involved for this essay. Little pearls of wisdom from their young minds, if you will. I thought, "This will be a great ending and show you guys how awesome homeschooling can be!"

I sat them down at the dinner table, that quintessential family bonding time. I asked what they like best about homeschooling, or if they had anything they wanted to say to parents who might be considering homeschooling. My nine-year-old moaned, "Do we have to do this now?" I swear, I have a teenager already. "Yes, I need your input."

He rolled his eyes. "Fine. I like doing my LEGO curriculum." My seven-year-old bounced up and down on her chair excitedly, "I like science and projects and roly polies and . . ." I broke in, reminding her that kids in public school do science and projects too.

Then my five-year-old threw his chair because I asked him to eat his chicken. The entire conversation ground to a halt when he managed to hit himself in the chin with his chair and bite his tongue hard enough to draw blood. The discussion was tabled and I tried not to laugh while comforting my distraught kiddo. Clearly, I have no pearls of wisdom from my kids to share.

Homeschooling is hard work, but so is every other good thing you'll ever attempt. Like parenting. If you can parent, you can homeschool. It's not about being an expert in everything but being an expert in your kid. You can find whatever resources you need for the educational part, but only you can do the part they need most—to be there for them.

That's the absolute best thing about homeschooling: being able to build a strong relationship bond with your kids, because you have all the time to do it.

14

ALEXIS DUFFIN

Alexis lives in Utah with her husband and their four children, ages two through eight. She has a bachelor's degree in Behavioral Science. She is an actor, teaches English to Chinese students, and is a member of The Church of Jesus Christ of Latter-day Saints.

ABOUT OUR FAMILY

Our family has been homeschooling from the beginning. We did Joy School for preschool with my oldest two and have kept things at home ever since. We are currently enrolled in an online charter school that supports homeschooling families. This allows us to be reimbursed for some home-school-related costs in exchange for simple weekly reports. The homeschool philosophy we most closely adhere to is "The Well-Educated Heart," promoted by Marlene Peterson. This philosophy focuses on priming children for self-driven learning with stories, music, art, and nature.

WHAT I LOVE ABOUT HOMESCHOOLING

When my oldest daughter was approaching kindergarten age, I attended my first homeschooling conference. My main objective was to figure out this: What was I supposed to do as a homeschooling mom? What was the long-term objective? If I could know the end-goal, then I could start to create the path.

Class after class didn't answer my questions. Even the workshop geared toward beginning homeschoolers didn't spell it out for me. The conference was almost over, and I had dozens of ideas of what I could make my path with, but I still didn't know where we were going or to what end. As I shuffled through the halls packed with moms who seemed like they knew what they were doing, I spotted one who had been on a panel I'd listened to earlier in the conference. Susan Van Cleave was a veteran homeschooling mother whose youngest child was starting his junior year. A small pressing feeling told me to talk to her, to ask her my big question. She graciously gave me a few minutes, and I asked her: "What are we even doing? What is the big overall goal we are working toward?"

Her answer resonated with me and has guided everything I've done for my children ever since. She told me that by the end of our children's "high school" education we want them to have the skills to be able to communicate and to be able to solve problems. It was so simple, and it was so profound. It was my answer. Now I could start—to choose from the endless ideas and schedules and philosophies and activities and organizations—to form the path to get us there.

Our family calls what we do "homeschool" because that's what makes sense to other people. But, really, we just live through our days, incorporating activities that strengthen communication and problem-solving skills. And we love it. The kids play. A lot. They play together; by themselves; with friends. We read. A lot. I read to them; they read to me, to each other, and to themselves; we listen to podcasts and audiobooks. We solve problems. Some of the problems are logic puzzles or math problems or about how things work. But we also spend a good amount of time working out the problems of life: how to get what we want; how to manage our time; how to deal with relationship struggles and big feelings. We work together on meals and on caring for the house and the yard. We spend time with people we love, including grandparents, cousins, friends, and neighbors. We have a few extracurricular activities. We have an involved, daily family devotional. And, we rest.

HOMESCHOOLING CHALLENGES

Now, that all sounds idyllic! At least it does to me. And there are brief moments where all goes as well as you could write it out on paper. But most of the time, it doesn't. A diaper needs to be changed and another kid is yelling on the toilet to be wiped at the same time. Someone gets hurt. A dish shatters on the floor. Someone took so-and-so's toy . . . again. Or mom just needs some precious alone time. Because, when you have little kids at home, they're constantly with you, and they need your attention. If you have to go somewhere, they all have to come, too. Any errand is a full-blown outing requiring everyone's shoes and a diaper bag and every child's request of something else we can do on that outing.

But, even if all is going according to plan, are you even working on the right plan? Are they challenged enough? Are they getting enough free time? Enough structure? Enough social time? Enough alone time? Enough time with you? Enough time with other mentors?

And, even if you feel like you've got the right plan, does your husband? Do your parents or in-laws?

The thing is, working through all these challenges helps me to improve *my* communication and problem-solving abilities. And beyond that, the challenges help me to look at each part of my full life and evaluate the worth of the activities, thoughts, and relationships that fill it. Through these challenges, I'm invited to discover how my children and I each think, our strengths, and how to help us each work through our unique difficulties.

PARTING WORDS

When I had my first conversation about homeschooling with a homeschooling friend, a small pressing feeling told me this path was worth exploring. That same small pressing feeling prompted me to talk to Susan Van Cleave and have a conversation that has defined my family's home-schooling journey. And the feeling continues to guide me in the steps we make part of our path to creating effective communicators and capable problem-solvers.

15

LM PRESTON

LM Preston is the author of Homeschooling and Working While Shaping Amazing Learners *and a homeschooling mother of four. She's an engineer, and a wife of more than twenty-five years. Her coaching and courses on homeschooling, college customization for homeschoolers or adults returning to school, and career reimagination, are products of her homeschooling journey. Homeschooling has enabled her kids to successfully complete college by the age of seventeen. In addition, she is a bestselling author of young adult fiction. She also writes for several small business publications focusing on women in business while parenting. Find her books and courses on www.EmpoweredSteps.com.*

ABOUT OUR FAMILY

Our family has lived in the Washington, DC and Maryland areas for most of our four kids' schooling. We've enjoyed the opportunities for work, the free museums, and the close distance to Virginia, Pennsylvania, Delaware, and New York. My husband and I both actively work full-time outside of the home while also homeschooling our kids. It has been a seven-year journey that has given us many challenges, but more rewards.

We started homeschooling when our youngest child was active and bored in school, and experienced teacher bullying in elementary school. He specifically requested to be homeschooled in second grade, and his sisters, in sixth grade and tenth grade, followed. Our oldest son was a traditional student who'd recently graduated from high school to attend a local community college.

Our approach to homeschooling as a working and homeschooling family has been rather unconventional. Both my husband and I have worked outside of the home since we started homeschooling. Childcare was our biggest hurdle, but with flip flopping our schedules, getting an in-home daycare provider for the hours no one was home, and doing school on nights and weekends, we made it work.

The curriculum choices we made were similar to traditional school since our kids requested to use the same curriculum. Also, my husband and I needed a structured program that was spelled out for us, so we could both share in the administering of school. The materials we used taught the lesson, provided workbooks that the kids could take with them when we traveled, and provided free online tutoring. We also supplemented with topics of interest selected and pursued by our kids. Our main goal was to shape our kids into independent learners whenever possible, and we did so by using various methods.

We homeschooled in math and English year-round through the use of spring and summer camps that focused on those topics, so our kids would be able to have a socialized learning experience over school break times. They were also able to explore their interests on their own throughout the year. They typically spent the majority of their springs and summers in camps. During the school year, in order for them to connect with various kids from diverse backgrounds in learning, they also participated in after-school programs offered by the state and other organizations.

Year-round schooling allowed our kids to condense the middle and high school years. By completing English and math requirements early, my kids were able to start college courses as early as age fourteen. Since they started dual enrollment programs at local community colleges or online colleges while finishing up high school, each of my three homeschooled children gained college degrees by the age of seventeen.

WHAT I LOVE ABOUT HOMESCHOOLING

Homeschooling has allowed us to customize the education of our children. Once we owned our freedom in homeschooling, we shaped it around our work schedules, and our kids thrived. We were able to scale up with activities and learning, and scale back to focus on areas where the kids needed to spend more time learning. We didn't move on to new topics within subjects until they mastered it, especially when it came to reading, writing, and math. Even though our biggest challenge was working outside of the home, we were forced to think outside the box and realize learning could happen in so many ways, at different times, and that the opportunities were boundless.

My son who was overactive and frustrated at school could now do his work on his own terms. It's allowed them to deep dive into topics of their own interest without having to shorten those discoveries due to other course obligations—we could build entire curriculums around a topic of their interest. It gave us a freedom we loved.

Even though many of our family and peers thought working and homeschooling was a crazy idea, my kids proved otherwise. It was the best journey we could have had with our kids. It allowed us to build stronger relationships and understanding of what works for each one of them. They have also gained the opportunity to learn on a larger scale than before—now that their learning has become personal.

HOMESCHOOLING CHALLENGES

The homeschooling challenge we met most was timing and coordination, since my husband and I both work full time.

We met this challenge by changing our schedules. My husband actually changed his career to one that allowed him the flexibility to work evenings and nights. Then when we found in-home daycare providers and nannies that would watch our kids, he transitioned back to his former career.

Kids are adaptable, and they adapted to our new schedule. Because they did school in the evenings with us, they slept later than before. They became more independent in their learning by tackling subjects on their own first. They sought answers on their own to get most of their work done, then asked us questions or for clarification when we were home from work. And we provided accountability and reviewed their work.

The other challenge was finding a peer group and socialization outlets for our kids. We had both an introvert and an extrovert, which made meeting their social needs seem daunting at first. Then we asked them what they wanted and needed in a social group. That helped us decide to enroll them in all the activities they'd done when attending traditional school. To them, it was the best part of school. Their activities weren't focused only on homeschool co-ops, events, and groups. They enjoyed being part of after-school camps, programs, and sports sponsored by local recreation programs or private organizations. Our kids thrived and gained friends from many backgrounds this way. Also, kids that were still connected with the traditional schools were great sources of information for activities that we wouldn't have otherwise known about.

PARTING WORDS

Working full time while homeschooling may seem impossible. However, anything is possible when you realize you have the freedom and flexibility to chart your child's own path to learning. Setting realistic expectations is always key. Bring your kid's voice to conversations about their learning—you may be surprised at how perceptive they are to their needs when asked.

16

MICHELLE HUDDLESTON

Michelle and her husband Bryan have homeschooled their five children going on seven years. Michelle is the author of Just for Today's Homeschooling Mom: A Whisper of Encouragement When You Need It Most, *and founder of the "Multi-Ethnic Homeschool Moms Conference." She resides in Western Kentucky (about an hour from Nashville) where she and her husband were both born and raised.*

ABOUT OUR FAMILY

Hey there Mom (and Dad)! My name is Michelle, I'm wife to my amazing husband Bryan, and we are the blessed parents of five incredible children.

Before homeschooling, I was a brick-and-mortar early childhood educator. I spent close to a decade teaching and tutoring children who were in their elementary years of learning. By the time our oldest son was in kindergarten, we decided to become homeschoolers.

Our choice stemmed from many reasons, some of which you can vouch for yourself. For starters, we noticed the turn for the worse public education was taking in regards to many of the concepts being taught, as well as the curriculum teachers were being forced to use. We also noticed an increase in classroom numbers which seemed to have led to more bullying and to teachers being overwhelmed. We wanted to ensure our one child (at the time), and any future children we would have, would be raised according to the principles, standards, morals, and values that we saw fit.

WHAT I LOVE ABOUT HOMESCHOOLING

That simple, but powerful, liberty is why I love homeschooling. Having the confidence to take my children's education into my own hands simply adds to it. I also love being able to take learning outside the box. It's amazing how a trip to the store can turn into a learning experience. But don't get me wrong, before understanding the different ways learning could take place, I was trapped in thinking it had to look a certain way to be perfect.

HOMESCHOOLING CHALLENGES

You see, being an ex-school teacher, I had many hurdles of my own to jump. Not only did I have a teacher mindset, but I also had a public school system mindset. It was embedded in me that school looked like waking up at a certain time every morning, starting school work by a certain time every day, and having subjects taught separately according to what was in the lesson plans. All of this had me subconsciously homeschooling with something that looked much like the school-at-home method.

I had the textbooks (I'm thankful for hand-me-downs), posters on the walls, and tables set up like desks. I also had the planners, lesson plans, and rigorous schedules. Little did I know that I didn't have to do all of those things as a homeschooler. Having a makeshift classroom didn't make me homeschool any better or any worse. Having detailed lesson plans didn't make my children learn any better. And teaching subjects separately didn't help me foster a love of learning in my children.

So, you're probably wondering what or if anything changed? The truth is I had to change. I had to change my perspective of what education and learning looked like. It wasn't my children's fault that Mommy would get frustrated, bogged down, or just plain exhausted trying to educate them at home. In most cases we want to immediately think something is wrong with our children, or that they somehow have the key to make this whole thing work if they only tried harder. I hate to say it, but that couldn't be further from the truth.

As a parent, I had to realize my responsibility and the role I play in making homeschooling work for our family. And once I figured that out, the rest is history.

Now our homeschool doesn't look much like school at all. Yes, I still have a few textbooks, I'll whip out a poster or two for reference, and my children love little workbooks that I pick up from the Dollar Tree. But other than that, our learning takes place all the time and in everything we do. Cooking becomes a fun science, math, and home economics lesson. Doing chores helps build character. And running errands becomes a lesson in life skills.

PARTING WORDS

When it comes to homeschooling, the possibilities truly are endless. I always encourage families to look at and embrace your own family dynamic, and use that to homeschool *your* way. Your journey should look just as unique as your family. Yes, there are styles, methods, and curriculum to navigate—but all that has its place. The best you can do is start slow, start small, and start simple. The rest will take care of itself.

I hope you have been encouraged by my story. If you need any assistance with getting started (and staying) homeschooling, please reach out to me. I have a blog with tons of resources and information at www.withthehuddlestons.com/blog and I also have a Facebook group: "Outta' Box Homeschooling." We are truly in this together!

17

FAYE BADENHOP

Faye is a homeschool mom and author of Help Me Homeschool!
*A former preschool owner, public school aide, and foster mother, she
is starting an organizing business—Organize, Minimize, Energize.
Married to a farmer, Faye is the mother of four—three grown children and a daughter who is graduating this year. Faye loves spending
time with her oldest son and his wife and children, traveling to Jackson Hole to see her artist daughter, playing ping pong with her other
son, taking her youngest to horse shows, healthy living, good coffee,
a good book, a relaxing winery with her husband, and Jesus.*

ABOUT OUR FAMILY

Life has a way of taking our plans and flipping them upside down and
then, looking back, we are so very grateful for the challenges that caused
the changes. I hadn't planned on being a homeschool mom. I had three
other children who had all graduated from public school. They were very
active in sports and other extra curriculars. All of them had made it to state
finals in different sports, a daughter was homecoming queen and salutato-
rian, they had friends coming and going, and life was good. But life was
quick. And life was busy. And family events got put to the side. Oh, I went

to everything I could go to, from chaperoning each field trip to volunteering at each PTO event, and attending and cheering wildly at every sporting event, spelling bee, and academic awards ceremony. It wasn't until the first child was getting ready to graduate from high school that I realized there were so many more things I had wanted to do with him. But my time was up. Life kept spinning, and soon the second and third were finished with high school and moving on.

By this time, I was also in the thick of foster parenting and had adopted a little girl who completed our family. But schoolwork didn't go as smoothly and easily for her as it did for my other children. She went to four years of preschool, and then started out in public school. She had excellent teachers in kindergarten, first, and second grades, but it was hard for her to get her work done in school. We spent all our spare time after school trying to accomplish her work. Towards the end of second grade, I realized that all she had time for, besides completing her schoolwork, was to eat, take a bath, and go to bed.

Shortly after that, it hit me that if we chose to homeschool, we would have an opportunity to learn while living. Instead of sitting in a classroom, which was not an atmosphere conducive to her way of learning, we could read books together in our treehouse, and she could learn the best way to take care of her animals by spending lots of time with them each day. I started making phone calls and asking questions. I began to get more and more excited about what I was hearing, and all the opportunities home-schoolers have. I quickly made the decision and have never looked back. Since homeschooling was not common in our area, I got many questions on how long we were going to homeschool. I would answer by saying that we were taking it one year at a time, but once we started, I knew, deep down, I could never go back. I loved it and she did too.

Getting advice from other homeschool parents, we ordered what she needed in each subject. I had no idea that there was such a wide variety of homeschool curriculum available. We went to our first homeschool convention in the spring of our first year and fell in love. Staying at a hotel with a pool couldn't even outshine the excitement and opportunities of learning from professionals and purchasing exciting products for the next school year. One of the hardest things was to say no to one curriculum in order to try another. We were never short on things we wanted to learn, and since it took my daughter longer to accomplish her assignments, we still spent many hours schooling. In that way we are different from many homeschool families, who accomplish their work quickly. Luckily for us, for the most part we never minded it. I would have to remind myself to let her, and myself, have breaks on the weekends.

WHAT I LOVE ABOUT HOMESCHOOLING

What I love most about homeschooling is the ability to tailor our daughter's education to her needs. Throughout our homeschooling years, some days learning consisted of doing only one subject. Other days, we completed many subjects, depending on how she was absorbing information that day. When we were learning something that she had no interest in, instead of spending lots of time on it, we would skim it and move on to her interests. That was very hard for me and took quite a while to adjust to. I felt obligated to totally finish each assignment. At our end of the year assessments, the sweet woman doing the assessing would remind me (every year) that I did not have to be an overachiever. I would still feel like there was so much more we could learn, but would then remind myself that every single thing does not have to be learned before high school graduation.

If you have ever been a parent of a public-school child, you may recall a project or two that your child needed to bring in, and although we knew better, we would tweak and advise and help "just a little" until they had this masterpiece for all the school to ooo and ahh over. Although this helped us get a little ego boost, it did nothing to help the child's creativity and brain power and self-esteem. Homeschooling has allowed me to let go of my competitive, perfectionist side and let her do projects in her way, to her ability. How much better to take a picture for her scrapbook of something that's her design rather than mine!

Lest you think you do not have it in you to give and give with nothing in return, let me remind you that you get to pick what you teach! Have you ever wanted to learn to decorate fancy cupcakes, do yoga, excel in a certain art or craft, or start an herb garden? Add it as a subject and you get to learn it too! Remember, there's a math lesson in everything. Take the subjects you didn't enjoy in school and make them interesting. I have learned more about history alongside my daughter than ever before, and now find it fascinating. And a lot of it we learned by reading fictional books and watching documentaries. Oh, and taking field trips! We have gone to places close by our home as well as across the country many times. Our backpacking trip to Central America was my daughter's favorite. How much easier learning can you get than that? You may be thinking that your housework will never get done when you are so busy teaching and doing all these extra activities, but remember that housework and laundry can be a subject. Mixing vinegar and baking soda to make not only a volcano, but a cleaner, and then researching why this happens, covers your science lesson and cleans the house all in one. Creativity cannot be topped when homeschooling. The sky is truly the limit!

If you are reading this, and about now are starting to think that my poor daughter needs to get away from her mother and get a little socialization, let me tell you about the co-op. Co-ops are a positive addition many homeschoolers take part in that allow them to get together to learn a wide variety of subjects and do interesting activities. The parents take part in the planning and teaching. At first, we didn't want to attend a weekly co-op since it took a lot of time to accomplish our home lesson plans. We started at a co-op that met twice a month, but after a year it closed because the leader was leaving and there was no one to take over. The second co-op we joined met once a week for about eight weeks a year, but after several years, it also closed because the leader moved on and there was no one to take her place.

This led us to our third and final co-op which meets each Friday throughout the school year. It has enabled my daughter to join singing groups with beautiful concerts twice a year, take part in homeschool musicals which are absolutely phenomenal (those homeschool kids can sing!), learn violin, and enjoy spring formals which were just as beautiful and well organized as any public-school proms I have helped put together. There are countless other activities to take part in including all kinds of sports with homeschool teams competing. They have their own graduation ceremony and last year's commencement speaker was racecar driver, Sam Hornish Jr.! Looking back, I second guess if we should have done the weekly co-op from the beginning because there are so many benefits. But I also believe that things happen for a reason and am very glad for the different opportunities we have had at the different co-ops, and my daughter is, too.

HOMESCHOOLING CHALLENGES

Being a perfectionist when my daughter is not has been one of our biggest challenges. Over the years, we both had to learn to compromise and not get frustrated with each other. When we would get frustrated, because frustrations when homeschooling can't be avoided, we took breaks from one another. She also needs study breaks often during the day, so when her mind drifts, it is time for her to do something active. Living on a farm, there are many opportunities for that. She can ride her horse, ride her bike, or head to the barn to learn how something mechanical works.

As you can tell, it takes a lot of time, energy, and commitment to homeschool. I have been fortunate that my husband is a good provider and I am pretty frugal, so I have not had to work full time as I homeschool. Small entrepreneurial jobs along the way have given us spending money as well as been a learning tool for my daughter. I have also been working on starting up an organizing business once she graduates. Homeschooling is a great time to get things ready so that when the day sneaks up on you when your last child graduates, you are not lost, but ready to move on with your own interests and dreams.

PARTING WORDS

Now as I am writing, big ol' tears are beginning to fall because this young daughter of mine is at the end of her senior year and we are getting ready for her graduation. Her cap and gown are hanging here in the kitchen, patiently awaiting the exciting day when she will put them on and we will celebrate what she has accomplished and anticipate what is to come. But the tears are not of regret. They are because I will so dearly miss our home-school days. I will miss the snuggles while reading, the races across the barnyard, the brainstorming together of what we were going to accomplish that day, that week, and that month. The giggles and the times she tells me how glad she is that I homeschooled her. I will even miss the arguments, the days when we didn't accomplish our goals, and the days when I told her it's time to go to public school because I couldn't take it anymore. It was hard but it was good. So good. And I am content. We made time for the important stuff. Do I wish I could go back and homeschool my older three children? No, because I believe everything happens for a reason. Would I go back and homeschool my youngest again? Absolutely!

18

HEIDI BULLARD

Heidi and her husband Josch are parents to five children, ages six through fourteen. They have been homeschooling for the past six years. After earning an associate degree, Heidi taught English and geography to underprivileged children in Guatemala. She loved the people and culture there and enjoyed traveling to many countries in Central America. Heidi is an active, fun-loving person who likes being with others. When she isn't busy homeschooling, she enjoys going on walks, riding her bike, reading, and serving in her community. Heidi and her family reside in Utah.

ABOUT OUR FAMILY

My husband and I both grew up attending public schools, and we never considered any alternatives to schooling. We were fine with sending our kids to a traditional brick and mortar public school. When our oldest child was old enough to go to kindergarten we enrolled her in all-day kindergarten. After she finished kindergarten, we heard about a new elementary school in our school district that was offering a Spanish Immersion program. We applied for the program and our two oldest kids were accepted. We were very excited about this.

117

Our kids attended this school for two years, participating in the Spanish immersion program and we loved everything about it. They made friends and we were happy with the administration and teachers. However, after two years of attending this school, we felt inspired to keep our kids at home and begin homeschooling instead. After much thought and prayer, we called the school in August, only three days before school was supposed to start, and told the principal that our kids wouldn't be coming back. Homeschooling was a journey that we had never considered embarking on, but we felt at peace with our decision and knew that we were being directed by God to do it.

Because my husband works outside our home and I stay home with the kids, it became primarily my responsibility to teach our kids. I had no idea how to go about homeschooling, but my children were young enough that I felt like I could take my time trying to navigate the homeschooling world and figure out what approach would be best for our family. The first couple of years homeschooling, we spent most of our time as a family reading a lot of books. The hardest thing to me about deciding to homeschool was that there were so many options. Just trying to figure out what curriculum to use for each child was so overwhelming. Thankfully, I was able to find other moms who were already homeschooling who gave me a lot of advice and resources to help.

We have now been homeschooling for six years and have homeschooled in a variety of ways. Currently, four of our kids go to charter schools one day a week and we get the majority of our curriculum from the schools that they attend. They do classes online and in person and this has been a good fit for a family. We are also part of a co-op and have joined a lot of other homeschooling groups in our community. Each year, my husband and I pray about what to do for the upcoming school year, evaluate all of our options, and decide what to do for the coming school year. Now that our kids are older, we also ask for their input and include them in our decision-making process. Our oldest child will be starting ninth grade this fall and is working toward a high school diploma. She also wants to earn an associate degree by the time she is done with high school and we will be working with the charter school she attends to make sure she is on track to achieve her goal.

WHAT I LOVE ABOUT HOMESCHOOLING

The thing I love the most about homeschooling is that I know what my children are being taught and I can help them learn the things that they are interested in learning. My kids have been able to take cooking classes, government and civics classes, hands-on science classes, dance and rock-climbing classes, and many others. I teach some subjects/classes at home, and I teach some classes in the community with kids from other families attending. When my kids want to learn something that I know nothing about, I find knowledgeable mentors and they teach my kids. I love that I am involved in what my kids are learning and that I can learn alongside them.

I also love that I get to be the person who spends the majority of every week with my children. Homeschooling is a huge commitment and it takes a lot of patience, but I am glad for the time that we have to spend together every single day. It is very rewarding to be able to see my children learn and progress and to know that I have played a huge role in that.

I also love the freedom to be able to create our own schedule during the day and to have family time each night. Instead of the stress of having hours of homework each night, we can get everything done that we need to each day, and then spend the evenings as a family doing fun things like playing sports. My kids also have time each day to play and explore the world, time to be bored, and free time in which to be creative.

HOMESCHOOLING CHALLENGES

There are many benefits to homeschooling, but there are also challenges. When we first started homeschooling, the biggest challenge I had was trying to get my kids to cooperate with doing their work. I have learned a lot over the years. I have learned to pick my battles. I've learned that it is okay to skip a day of math or spelling because one of my children is struggling and needs a break. I've found that the more my kids feel like they are in charge of their learning, the less of a struggle it is to get them to be engaged in their work each day. My kids have learned to enjoy learning and I no longer feel like I am forcing them to learn.

Recently, the biggest struggle that I've had with homeschooling is finding the time to teach five different kids many different subjects and on five different grade levels. I have had to learn to manage my time wisely and to prioritize what is most important in my life. And I have had to learn to avoid distractions from things that don't really matter. Homeschooling takes up a good portion of time each day, but it is manageable, even with five kids.

PARTING WORDS

I do not hesitate to recommend homeschooling to any family who is wanting to try it. My advice to families who are just starting to homeschool is to jump in with both feet and get started. Find others who already homeschool who can be a support and who can give you help and ideas. However, your way of homeschooling will not look like their way of homeschooling. There is no one right way of doing it. That is the beauty of homeschooling. Each family gets to choose what is best for their family. What is best for my family has changed from time to time and that is okay too. Although homeschooling is not easy and isn't always fun, I have never regretted the decision to homeschool. I am glad for the time that homeschooling has given me to teach my children. I am thankful for the guidance that God gave my husband and me to begin homeschooling six years ago. I have learned a lot throughout our homeschooling journey and wouldn't trade it for anything.

19

GLENN BALLARD

Glenn grew up in Alabama, and now lives in Silicon Valley, California. Glenn is Caucasian, and his wife, Pearl, is Chinese, and grew up in Taiwan. Together, they homeschool their four children, ages eight, thirteen, fourteen, and fifteen, all of whom were born in California.

ABOUT OUR FAMILY

My wife, Pearl, has an undergraduate degree in engineering, which she obtained in Taiwan, and two master's degrees in education, which she earned in the United States. I have undergraduate degrees in engineering and accounting and master's degrees in finance, tax, and business, including an MBA from the University of California, Berkeley. My wife and I both attended public schools throughout our entire educational processes.

We are Christians, and teaching our children to love and fear the Lord is the most important priority in our parenting, including our decision to homeschool. When we got married, my wife was a teacher at a highly regarded public high school. But we both knew there was no way we would ever send our children to public school, because we didn't want them to be indoctrinated with atheism and Darwinism, and we didn't want them bombarded with moral hazards such as drugs, sex, and temptations to abuse alcohol. In other words, we wanted to protect our children, as all parents should. So, from the very beginning, our choice was between Christian private schooling or homeschooling.

I was first introduced to the concept of homeschooling when I was a college student in Atlanta in the early 1980s when a guest speaker came to my church to talk about it. This was when homeschooling was still very rare and considered "fringe." I thought to myself, "That's a great idea!" But it would be about twenty years before I would have my own children and therefore need to seriously consider the option of homeschooling.

I taught all four of our children to read English, beginning with phonetics, when they were each between the ages of three and four years old. My mother taught me to read, and so I was confident that I could also teach my own children to read. It was more difficult than I had imagined it would be, but we were able to persevere, and all of my children learned to read at young ages, well before first grade and even kindergarten. I also taught them beginning math concepts, like counting and simple addition and subtraction at early ages.

When the time came for our oldest child to start first grade, we sort of glided into homeschooling without a lot of analysis. Our first daughter was very shy at six years old. I felt strongly that, "My baby is not ready to go to school," and, "I'm not ready to send my baby to school." I talked with my pastor at the time, who was homeschooling his children, and who also was well educated and a very reasonable, sensible person. He calmed my fears and doubts about homeschooling. So, we forged ahead. We planned to take homeschooling one year at a time, with the idea that at some point along the way, we'd probably move to traditional private Christian school.

The first year did not go well. I was overconfident and plunged in without a well-thought-out plan or system. I bought a couple of math and reading comprehension books from a local school supply store, but I didn't put nearly as much thought and planning into it as I should have. My wife was very upset with me that first year. She was worried I was ruining our children's lives.

At the end of my first daughter's first-grade year, we attended a home-school convention in our area, which was tremendously encouraging to my wife and tremendously helpful to our family. My wife was able to meet many other homeschooling moms and families and even witness some out-standing older homeschooling students who had turned out well. This greatly calmed her fears. Also, there were publishers of homeschool curric-ula there who were presenting and selling their textbooks and other materials. Wow! We had no idea there were so many resources available! We bought some excellent textbooks and other resources and were able to pursue a much more well-planned, well-thought-out, systematic approach to homeschooling from then on.

My oldest daughter is now fifteen. We have completed nine years of homeschooling. Our approach is referred to as the classical, Christian edu-cation model. Our children study religion (including historical confessions and catechisms), math, natural sciences, languages (English, Latin, Hebrew, Greek, and Spanish), history, logic, and music (currently, piano and music theory). They also participate in speech and debate (I coach their speech and debate club). And, as they are getting older, we are adding things like computer programming and other technology courses. We are now fully committed to homeschooling all the way through high school and never have a thought of putting them in a typical school, either public or private.

For our first eight years of homeschooling, we were mainly at home, with limited outside activities, which included church attendance, debate tournaments, and piano lessons and recitals. In our ninth year of home-schooling (the ninth, eight, and seventh grades of our three older children), we greatly expanded our outside activities to include Classical Conversa-tions (a national homeschool co-op program that provides a structured classical Christian education); HEART Academy (a local homeschool co-op that provides science and technology classes); and Lux Debate.

I mentioned previously that our number one priority is to train our children to love and fear God. That remains our top priority and value. However, we also have a secondary value—academic excellence. We expect our children to pursue and attain excellence in academics. Our goal is for them to be well-educated, well-trained, academically excellent students, who will be able to exert a positive influence in the world, and that our family will generate a multigenerational heritage of producing many strong Christians and citizens, who will influence the world for good for decades and centuries into the future.

WHAT I LOVE ABOUT HOMESCHOOLING

There are so many things I love about homeschooling. It's really impossible to name them all. But here are a few. I love that my children study religion, in a serious academic manner. I love that my children love to study and love to learn, that they have not been trained to dislike learning by an unhealthy school environment. I love that my children are developing critical thinking skills and learning to think for themselves, and they do not merely accept every idea of currently popular opinion (some of which are completely nonsensical). I love that my children understand that biological life appears designed because it is designed.

I love that my children are voracious readers. I love that my twelve-year-old son, who is academically advanced by two or three grades, is able to excel and advance and work at his level of ability, and not be held back by a public school system that dumbs things down to teach to the average student in the class. I love that my children are able to participate in wonderful and enriching activities like debate and speech tournaments and mock trial (similar to moot court) competitions.

I love that my children love each other and are close to each other. I love that the members of my family are able to see each other and interact with each other and be with each other much of the day, every day, rather than just a few hours at night and on the weekends. I love that my children are not sleep deprived. I love that my children are healthy and happy. I love that my children are not exposed to sex and drugs much younger than is healthy for any child. I love that my family can set our own schedule, for the most part, most days, and we are not slaves to a school bell or schedule. I love that we can go snow skiing in the mountains or to the beach during the middle of the week, when those places are not crowded. I love that my children are not subjected to the tremendous amount of foolishness and nonsense that happens in public schools, perpetrated not only by other students, but also by some textbooks, teachers, and administrators.

HOMESCHOOLING CHALLENGES

Homeschooling is hard; there's no doubt about that. But it's worth it. It's so worth it. Homeschooling is hard in the same way that parenting is hard. But there are many excellent resources to help you homeschool, including many online resources.

One obvious challenge with homeschooling is scheduling. If both mama and daddy are busy with long hours in the office in high-powered, highly demanding careers, homeschooling becomes nearly impossible. Arranging a family schedule that allows for homeschooling requires sacrifice on the part of mama or daddy or both. From the time our first child was born, my wife made the sacrifice to give up her career and be a stay-home-mom—the most important job in the world. I will always be grateful for her sacrifice, and it has been a tremendous blessing to our children. I have my own business, and I am able to work from home most days, and I also am very involved with our children's homeschooling.

I understand that not all parents are able to arrange their schedules and times like we have. But I also know that, even though it can be very difficult, parents who earnestly desire to homeschool tend to find a way to do it. We have known Chinese parents who could barely speak English find a way to homeschool their American-born, English-speaking children by using videos and online resources and by pooling together resources with other friends to help each other. The most difficult circumstance for home-schooling, I think, is the situation of a single-parent family. I can't imagine how hard that must be. And yet, we know a single mother who home-schools her children, with the help of other families from church, as well as the broader homeschool community.

Homeschooling families love to help other homeschooling families. So, for the single parent, or the families for which both parents must work outside the home, if God has put the desire to homeschool your children in your heart, I would encourage you to strive to find a way, including asking other families for help. Homeschooling families helping other homeschool-ing families has a long and honorable history in the United States, going all the way back to the community schoolhouses in the New Plymouth Plan-tation colony.

PARTING WORDS

When I was asked to write this essay about homeschooling, I was eager to do it, even though I am extremely busy, because I am fully persuaded of the tremendous value and wonderful blessing of homeschooling, and I am passionate about encouraging as many other parents as possible to also homeschool their children. I understand that the prospect of homeschool-ing, if you are considering it for the first time, can seem daunting, to say the least. Perhaps overwhelming or seemingly impossible would be more accu-rate descriptors. At the very beginning of our homeschooling journey, I read something very helpful that I would like to pass along to you now. If you can parent, you can homeschool. Homeschooling is simply parenting x 10 (or maybe x 100 some days). If you want to do it, you can do it. And you are uniquely qualified and equipped to homeschool your children, *be-cause they are your children.*

Outsourcing some tasks is an effective strategy for many businesses. My own business outsources services to companies. Outsourcing provides a compelling value proposition in many different circumstances. But parent-ing is not one of them. Outsourcing the care, education, and training of our children is a huge mistake.

People who say, "You can have it all," are mistaken. We all have to choose what is most important and sacrifice things of lesser importance. Very sadly, too many parents are deceived into thinking their careers are the most important priority in life and that the care, education, and training of their children should be outsourced. The big losers from this sort of arrangement are the children. The secondary loser is society at large, which is suffering from way too many adults who did not receive proper moral and religious training when they were children and adolescents.

In the Bible, in Deuteronomy, chapter six, the Lord commands parents to *diligently* teach his commandments to their children. This command still stands today. Nothing in the world is more important. We will be held accountable to God for training our own children. The excuse that, "They weren't teaching that in my child's school," will not cut it.

Homeschooling is hard (most of the best things in life are), but it's worth it. It's the most important thing you can do with your life. Do it for your children. Do it for the Lord. Do it for the world.

20

THERESA REDFERN-HALL

Theresa graduated from a women's liberal arts college with a bachelor's in Paralegal Studies and has worked as a legal assistant, an advocate for battered women, a court reporter and bailiff for county court judges, and a volunteer coordinator for a women's shelter. Theresa and her spouse live in South Minneapolis with their three children ages twenty-four, twenty-two, and twenty. Her household also includes a huge dog, a tiny dog, and cats. Her motto for life and learning is "Question everything."

ABOUT OUR FAMILY

We began the homeschooling journey shortly after our first child was born in 1995. Having been raised in rural southern Indiana, where everyone I knew went to our local school on the school bus and lived and breathed high school basketball, homeschooling was not even in my vocabulary until after graduating from college. At that point, I thought homeschooling was an anomaly only entered into by people trying to stay off the radar—people with something to hide.

My partner mentioned the idea of homeschooling to me as I sat on the couch, our three-week old daughter cradled in my arms, watching a local news broadcast. The lead story was about a first-grade student who had been killed in a school bus accident. I held my child a bit tighter as I watched the reporter relay the story. My partner walked out of the kitchen, looked at us and said, "You know, homeschooled kids don't get hit by school buses." That was the launching point for a multi-year homeschooling adventure.

To say that I was an immediate convert to the idea of homeschooling would be a lie. I loved working outside our home. I enjoyed my job, my work friends, and interacting with the public. I was in a position where I did community education and trained volunteers. It was fun and exciting to go to work. However, when we decided to have more children, we also decided I would stay home and take care of the kids. Two more children followed our first. Soon, we had three children under the age of four and the more time I spent with them, the more I realized I didn't want to send them off, to someone else, to spend the best part of the day with them. The thought of homeschooling became more appealing.

I am an organizer. I enjoy planning things out to the smallest detail and my calendar was detailed. Having officially made the decision to homeschool, I read lots of books about raising a classically trained child and it appealed to me. I planned out daily lessons beginning in preschool. We would have an organized homeschooling journey; our homeschooling school day would follow a traditional bricks and mortar school day without wasting time for classroom management. That was my plan. My kids taught me a different way.

Each of my children have very different personalities and learning styles. I quickly learned from them that my planned, one-size-fits-all approach would not fit them. We eventually settled upon an eclectic style of homeschooling. Through interactions with a local co-op group, we participated in structured activities. With a smaller group of homeschooling friends, we created a study-group of four families. With this group, we met on a weekly or bi-weekly basis. The parents worked together to develop the learning activities and present it to the children. We went to the orchestra, plays, and dance recitals. We participated in historical events and science projects and many other learning opportunities with this group of homeschooling friends. We always laughed when well-meaning strangers would ask us about socialization for the children. There were times when I actually wanted less socialization, just to be able to stay home. So many of those families continue to be lifelong friends—not only the children, but the parents too.

My oldest is very artistic and a visual learner. When I added an art or creative element to any lesson, she flourished and enjoyed the learning. However, she also is an introvert who needs time to sit back, observe people, and then make a decision about how she wants to interact with them. As an adult, she continues to do the same.

My son taught himself to read when he was five years old. I hadn't set out to teach him to read at the time. He surprised us when he brought a chapter book to the dinner table and sounded out the name of the book, "*Space Race.*" I remember thinking, "Well okay then, here we go with him." He was fascinated with how things worked. He enjoyed taking things apart and putting them back together again. When we would go to the zoo, he would spend a good deal of the time investigating anything mechanical that was located near the exhibits. Currently, he's looking at becoming an electrician.

Our third child is an experiential learner and driven by relationships. She never meets a stranger, and really enjoys meeting new people and traveling. She has always pushed boundaries and isn't happy until she actually participates, learning by doing. She learned to read much later than her siblings, but like her older sister, she loves art. She was also my first child to decide she wanted to go to a school outside of the house. She approached me one day and said, "Well Mom, I need to learn things and I won't listen to you, so I need to have a teacher that isn't you." We compromised, and she went to a school that met in person three days a week and was online two days a week. She is still pushing boundaries today. She's attending college for political science and wants to work with disadvantaged persons. Her study abroad program was in Cuba and she had to lobby her university to have the program included.

WHAT I LOVE ABOUT HOMESCHOOLING

When the kids were younger, we would spend a portion of the spring and fall traveling and camping. During our trips, we knew that we would be able enjoy many of the attractions without competing with non-homeschooling families, many of whom try to cram in family time during the limited breaks offered by schools. Because of our flexible schedule, we were also able to spend more time with my mother, prior to her death. When we found out she was ill, we could just pick up and go without worrying about pulling the kids from school.

It was wonderful to have the ability to let the kids direct their learning. If they were fascinated with owls, we learned about owls. If we read a book about Louisiana, we learned everything we could about living there. We followed their interests. I also appreciated that if the kids didn't feel well, I didn't need to worry about getting them to school so they didn't miss classes or tests. They could be at home, let the virus run its course, and not infect others.

We were so fortunate to have those extra years of homeschooling with our children. We were able to watch their personalities develop, their days unfold, and experience life with them. We didn't just hear about what happened when they came home after school. We learned who they were and how they made decisions. I think this really helped us as they became young adults. We weren't caught off-guard by perceived personality changes.

HOMESCHOOLING CHALLENGES

All this is not to say that there weren't challenges in our homeschooling journey. We went from a two-income family down to a one-income family.

At times, money was a real issue for us. It helped us to acknowledge that we had made a conscious decision to take this path and live this lifestyle. We persevered and made it through financially tight times.

Another challenge we faced was that my oldest child and I are very alike. We look similar and think in similar ways. We clashed as she got older. This dynamic is not uncommon in families, but we were together 24/7. We had the usual parenting challenges of sibling fights, bedtime, and what vegetables needed to be eaten.

We also had the challenge of not fitting into the general societal mold of heading off to kindergarten, and explaining this choice over and over to concerned extended family members and strangers who questioned why our children weren't in school. We needed to be very proactive about searching out families that held a similar view and philosophy.

Another challenge we faced was giving our children permission to decide when it was time for them to go to school outside of our home. Occasionally, they also decided it was time for them to come back to homeschooling for a bit, and then head off to traditional school again.

PARTING WORDS

So, is homeschooling worth the effort? In my opinion, yes. You can choose to send your child off to school and let others work with your child for nine months of the year. There are many great schools out there and wonderful teachers who are devoted to working with students. We have met and know many of these individuals. We were educated in these types of schools. However, I truly believe that homeschooling is worth every effort and every bad day you might have in your journey. Because that is what homeschooling is—a journey. It's being able to spend incredible time with your children, it's being able to watch them learn and, in turn, learn from them. It gave all of us an expanded opportunity to build trust within our family. We formed relationships with our children that allowed them to trust us. We also learned to trust them and their decisions. We respect each other. And while we may not agree with every decision being made, we respect that our children will be able to handle those decisions and learn from the decisions they made. I loved that I was able to spend this extra time with my children.

I believe so much in homeschooling that I have continued to work with families who are taking on the homeschooling life. Currently, I am privileged to teach homeschool students at two local co-ops. I've been teaching at one of those co-ops since 2008. I enjoy the ability to get to know new students each year. I am able to share my passion for homeschooling and teach about subjects I love. Each of the students I teach is so unique and I really do consider it to be a privilege to work with them and their parents. Like my own adventure in homeschooling my children, I go into each class I teach with a plan, but depending on the students I have in those classes, I am flexible and make it work for each student.

Learning takes place throughout your life. If you can spend a few fleeting years with your children learning new things or relearning old things, take advantage of that opportunity. As I mentioned before, homeschooling is a journey. Take that journey with your children. Don't worry about when to get off the homeschool train, just enjoy the wonderful time with your kids. They grow so fast and you will never get the time back again.

21

LISA KENDALL

Lisa is married to Justin, the man of her dreams, and they have six children (so far), ages ten months to ten years. They married thirteen years ago and have lived in ten different states. They have been mostly homeschooling for the past five years, and for the past year have been 100% homeschooling for the first time. Her family likes playing card games and taking the scenic route on long drives. Lisa enjoys the beach, going to the YMCA, reading, and hosting play-dates for the kids.

ABOUT OUR FAMILY

My husband and I recently celebrated our thirteenth year of marriage by buying our first home, in Virginia, making it our twenty-first move. We are looking forward to finally being able to plant some roots! We have six kids: a girl, age ten, and five boys, ages nine, seven, three, two, and almost one.

I didn't do so well in school. I would study like crazy for a test and still get a C, if I was lucky. I used to base my feelings of self-worth on my grades and how much education I received . . . or didn't receive. I still haven't finished a semester of college. I have since learned that, while education is very important, God doesn't base our value on our level of education. I am grateful for that. I have also learned that there is a lot more to education than grades and degrees.

Because I didn't come to love learning until after high school, when I became a mother, I wanted to instill in my kids a love of learning early on. Despite lacking a college education, I feel God planted in my heart, long before we had kids, a desire to homeschool. Due to lacking confidence in myself, my oldest has actually been in and out of public school, and another of my kids attended a semester of kindergarten. But gradually I have gained more confidence in myself and let go of others' expectations. I know more about my children and their individual strengths, weaknesses, and needs than any teacher, and I am the person in the best position to provide an individualized education to my children.

I have also realized that homeschooling parents don't need to know everything in order to be able to do an awesome job teaching their children. More importantly, homeschooling parents need to be willing to help their children be curious about the world, ask questions, and seek answers. When my children ask me something I don't know, we find out together. We look things up and read a lot.

Because of my new-found confidence, this year we homeschooled all of our children, and we plan to continue on this path.

I've used a lot of quotes in this chapter because I feel that those who I quote perfectly communicate exactly how I feel. I really relate to the style of homeschooling Durenda Wilson describes in the book, *The Unhurried Homeschooler*. I'll share a few examples.

What unhurried homeschooling is not:

- *Refusing to give directions or have order or routine*
- *Refusing boundaries or expectations*
- *Turning a blind eye to character issues*
- *Ignoring state laws regarding homeschooling*
- *Letting our kids run amuck*

- *Refusing to challenge our kids to try things they think they can't do*
- *Refusing to make them do things they don't want to do . . .*[1]

Wilson describes what unhurried homeschooling looks like:

- *Allowing our children to learn at their own pace . . .*
- *Being tuned in to when our children are ready to learn something, when they are not, and following through when they are*
- *Willing to be flexible*
- *Being more concerned with what is best for our children than what makes us feel good or look successful . . .*
- *Remembering who we are and the example we set. How we approach life, handle stress, our world view, etc. will have a greater impact on our children than any curriculum or bookwork*[2]

My motto is, "They are only little for so long," so I encourage lots of play and use of their imaginations.

Besides play, my kids help out a lot around the house, which teaches them important skills that prepare them for when they are grown and will have their own families and homes. We do some workbook activities throughout the week. I use an online program to help my seven-year-old learn how to read. I do my best to read to my kids daily. We also like to watch documentaries on a variety of subjects. My daughter and I love to draw, so we do art projects together throughout the week. Sometimes they help me with baking projects. What kid doesn't love that? They could play LEGOs with each other for hours upon hours. We go on walks, and enjoy trips to the beach, and simply spending time together (for the most part, anyway). The opportunity to learn at home is endless.

WHAT I LOVE ABOUT HOMESCHOOLING

Boyd K. Packer, a spiritual leader and former school teacher said, "In many places it is literally not safe physically for youngsters to go to school. And in many schools—and it's becoming almost generally true—it is spiritually unsafe to attend public schools."[3]

I love knowing that my kids are at home and safe. I won't always be able to protect them from everything, and heaven knows we all have enough trials as it is, but again, they are only so little for so long and I want to experience life with them while they are still living under our roof. I feel that this quote by Marisa Boonstra sums it all up:

> People often say to me, 'You can't keep your children in a bubble.' And I reply, 'It's not a bubble, it's a greenhouse.'
> A bubble stifles growth and blocks out nutrients. A greenhouse provides an environment for cultivation.
> Children's hearts need to be 'greenhoused' before they're ready to be transplanted out into the world. We release when their roots are deep and they are mature enough to withstand the storms, not beforehand. While they're still under our protection, we take the responsibility for engaging them in learning about different cultures, ideologies, and values. . . .
> It's neither parenting out of fear or legalism, nor going to the opposite extreme of being too permissive.
> No, our kids shouldn't grow up in a bubble. But they shouldn't be left exposed to the harsh outside elements, either.
> The greenhouse of our home has all the right conditions for those young seeds to grow and flourish.[4]

Part of what I love about homeschooling is what we *don't* have to do. We don't have to wake up early to catch the bus. I don't have to worry about preparing snacks and lunches for them to take to school. We don't have to deal with homework after they have already been gone all day. We don't have to do fundraisers for the school. We don't have to deal with curricula we don't agree with. And we don't have to put up with bullying. I love that my kids get to grow up together and be best friends (when they aren't fighting).

HOMESCHOOLING CHALLENGES

Clashing personalities is probably the hardest part of homeschooling for our family. I have two kids who fight with each other like cats and dogs.

Sometimes I wonder if it would be better for us to not all be together all of the time, but I know God wouldn't have planted this idea to homeschool in my heart and so strongly if it weren't for the best. I trust that He sees the bigger picture.

It can also be a little challenging to have a baby and toddlers while trying to work with the older kids, and honestly, I don't have that part figured out yet. As Diane Hopkins says,

> 'The baby IS the lesson!' I thought I was trying to teach math, but in reality I had been teaching, day by day, how an adult values the precious gift of children. My children, by watching how I deal with the frustration of a crying baby or keep a toddler happy and busy with some of his 'own' pieces while we play a math game, are soaking up 'the lesson.'[5]

My mom likes to remind me, "You're doing better than you think."

Another big challenge is simply dealing with my own insecurities. But I know that God qualifies those He calls and I know that I was called to homeschool. Another quote that speaks to my soul is, "Don't shy away from something that the Lord is trying to lead you to because you feel afraid, inadequate, or unprepared. When God says it is time, it *is* time! When He says you are ready, you *are* ready."[6] Homeschooling is my greatest opportunity to exercise faith and to trust in the Lord.

PARTING WORDS

I don't need to know everything. I love my kids very much and the Lord will make up for what I lack. He guides me and somehow it all works out.

If you feel called to homeschool, I hope you take the leap of faith and do it. God will help you!

¹ Durenda Wilson, *The Unhurried Homeschooler*, 2016, 36. Permission to use granted by Durenda Wilson.

² Durenda Wilson, *The Unhurried Homeschooler*, 2016, 35. Permission to use granted by Durenda Wilson.

³ Boyd K. Packer, October, 1996. Quoted in Connor Boyack, *Latter-day Liberty* (Cedar Fort, 2011), 205.

⁴ Marisa Boonstra, "I'm Not Raising My Kids in a Bubble, I'm Raising Them in a Greenhouse," *Her View From Home: Stories From the Heart of Every Home.* Accessed June 20, 2020 at http://www.herviewfromhome.com/kids-greenhouse. Permission to use granted by Marisa Boonstra.

⁵ Diane Hopkins, "The Baby Is the Lesson," *Love to Learn.* Accessed June 20, 2020 at https://www.lovetolearn.net/most-important-homeschool-lesson.

⁶ Author unknown. Shared at https://www.facebook.com/Walkbyfaithandnotbysight.

22

CARA RECTOR

Cara has five daughters ages three to eighteen. Cara and her husband Russ have been homeschooling their children for nine years. Cara herself was homeschooled off and on through high school. She has an associate degree from Southern Virginia University. She is heavily involved in the planning and execution of homeschooling conferences that support and uplift fellow homeschooling families.

ABOUT OUR FAMILY

I am from a small but growing group of homeschooling parents who were themselves homeschooled as children. As a result, I began my homeschool with some experience under my belt.

Each of our daughters has very different goals and talents. We refer to our homeschooling style as "patchwork." We stitch together many different types of curriculum in order to best meet each of our children's individual needs.

I grew up in a military family. So I know well how to duck and pivot around ever-changing life circumstances. But, as always seems to be the case, I had more to learn.

141

My husband and I had four beautiful daughters, all born between 2002 and 2008. As homeschoolers, we've had our fair share of struggles and triumphs. It took a solid three years of homeschooling to feel confident that we were headed in the right educational direction. There were many long days and short weeks. We were happy with our circumstances. We were growing.

When our oldest was thirteen years old, I started feeling a small nudge. That clichéd feeling that someone was missing. I felt it, and dismissed it, for a long time. Eventually, I came to learn that my husband, Russ, was having the same experience. So, our hearts softened and we decided that adding another child to our family was a blessing we didn't want to pass up.

All of my previous pregnancies had been rough and we knew this one would likely be harder. I decided to focus on the excitement instead of worrying about the "what ifs." I became pregnant, and was due in June 2015. Our previous youngest was turning eight shortly after the baby would arrive. Then the scene changed on a dime when I went in for my fourteen-week ultrasound. Things weren't right. We discovered that I was miscarrying. I was headed down the road of learning the beauty of living in "survival mode."

Several blurry months later, I decided I could try for a new child one last time. I was willing to leave my heart open to the possibility of one more. I became pregnant again. Things progressed well. Given my history of preeclampsia, we knew that it was likely to set in midway through my third trimester, but we felt prepared for that. We did not, however, feel prepared when we learned I had preeclampsia at twenty-five weeks. And our new baby girl was measuring too small. Both of those together meant I would live in the hospital for several weeks.

I had no idea how to manage homeschool from a distance. Our style of homeschooling had worked in the past because I was there to manage things. I had a sense of being in control, at least to an extent. The infant loss had shaken that deeply. When I developed preeclampsia during this pregnancy, any remaining illusions I felt of having control over my life were swept away. It was painful but beautiful. The gift of living in "survival mode" for us lies in how it reveals the most important things. I have always pored over finding the right homeschool curriculum for my children. Trying, failing, and trying again to create a routine. Working to provide the best learning environment that balances challenging the kids while not overwhelming them. Now they had to fly solo. Russ was able to work from home but couldn't be as hands-on as I had been.

I was admitted to the hospital in such a way that there was no time for preparation. Then, the Lord began teaching us all in ways we never knew we needed. My situation stabilized enough that we could wait to deliver. We ended up making it to thirty-two weeks. This was an absolute miracle because everyone, doctors included, thought we would be lucky to reach twenty-eight weeks.

During my hospitalization, schoolwork habits shifted a lot. The kids focused on language arts and math. And they spent the day playing on screens more than I wanted them to. Russ drove them around to their activities. And they came to visit me every night after dinner. We all received a very real first-hand lesson in being willing to accept help, as our church stepped in with a robust meal plan, providing meals for our family for well over a month. Nothing in our lives during this time was normal, but oh, was it beautiful.

WHAT I LOVE ABOUT HOMESCHOOLING

Sweet lessons were learned during my pregnancy. A few that stand out are as follows:

- Our oldest remembers being amazed at seeing our family's "cup running over," as so many meals were brought to our home.
- Our second daughter learned to take up the mantle of doing the laundry, and she ran with it.
- Our third daughter learned that hard is doable.

- Our fourth daughter learned that miracles happen and hospitals aren't scary.
- I learned that while my family is mine, these sweet humans are not made nor broken by me.

Our new youngest is now a healthy, headstrong toddler. She is a delight and a trial to her teen sisters. Which is how it should be.

HOMESCHOOLING CHALLENGES

It's always a challenge to meet the unique learning needs of multiple children. When life steps in and changes our plans, that makes it even harder. I was so worried that our kids would fall behind. Even more, I was worried that they would be less willing to work hard when they were under less supervision during my hospital stay. I feared there would be gaps in their education. We still face many of these challenges. We are still figuring things out. But none of the kids have fallen behind.

Learning scholastic things will come. Learning hard things will come. Both are messy. Both are beautiful. Growth is ever present throughout life.

PARTING WORDS

I love so many things about our wild and wonderful homeschool journey. As I watch my children blossom into adulthood, my fears are subsiding. They have learned precious lessons that have prepared them for life. I will forever be grateful for the gift of our seasons living in "survival mode."

23

ANN BARNDT

Ann and her husband have three sons, ages twenty-three, twenty, and twelve. They have been home educating their children for almost two decades. Ann has a bachelor's degree in Computer Science from Rochester Institute of Technology and was a software engineer before embarking on a career as a homeschool mom. She teaches computer science at her local homeschool co-op, has helped run speech and debate tournaments for homeschoolers, and is an avid birdwatcher. She currently resides in the Boston, Massachusetts area, but you can also find her at www.barndt.org.

ABOUT OUR FAMILY

My husband and I have always known that our children were gifts from God. We are Christians and want to be faithful to God in all things, including raising the children He has given us. Proverbs 22:6 says, "Train up a child in the way he should go; and when he is old, he will not depart from it" (The New King James Version). We decided together early on that we would take responsibility for our children's education. Eventually, we even gave a name to our little homeschool: "The HI Road Academy"—"H" for Humility and "I" for Integrity. We wanted these traits to be at the root of the journey we were on together. While we had academic aspirations for our children, we always had the following big-picture goals in mind:

Before leaving school, the student shall be equipped to

- Contribute to the worship of God
- Know his way around the Bible
- Think and reason
- Initiate and complete projects
- Solve problems
- Form his own opinions
- Resist temptation
- Seek God's will for his life
- Practically live on his own
- Pursue further education in the area of his choice
- Recognize and participate in the creation of beauty

And others shall recognize that he is

- Well-rounded
- Well-spoken
- Well-traveled
- Well-read
- Well-mannered

WHAT I LOVE ABOUT HOMESCHOOLING

We have a plant in our front yard called a clematis. It's set at the base of a light post and every spring it sends out runners. In July it blooms with great big purple flowers which have wonderful curb appeal if I train the runners upward.

The key is timing and gentleness. The runners grow so fast, if I don't deal with them, they will just end up entangled at the base of the post. If I tie the runners to the pole and adjust the ties as they grow, eventually I'll end up with dozens of flowers scattered around the pole and encircled about the light. I can't tie the stems too tightly to the pole or I'll break the runner. Loosely tying them to the pole and allowing them to naturally inch their way upward gives the best results.

Our children are the same way. The rapid growth when they are young can be trained upward and outward to where they can do the most good. But this training must be provided gently and at the right time.

What I love most about homeschooling is having the freedom and flexibility to guide my children as they grow. All children grow at their own natural pace. By homeschooling, I can see pretty quickly if an adjustment needs to be made. I can support them so they can grow up in a way that makes the most sense for them.

Throughout our homeschool journey, one of the supports we give them is prayer. What's best for them? How does the Lord want to use them? What are their natural abilities that He wants to use for His service? For one child it was geography, computers, and visual arts. For another, it was planes, birds, and competitive debate. The third is still young, but he has already demonstrated a natural gift for music and composition.

The beauty of homeschooling is that we were and are able to provide a personalized education for each of them. An Individualized Education Program (or an IEP) is typically only created for students with learning difficulties. Why? Why shouldn't all kids get an IEP? I picture Oprah pointing at her audience: "You get an IEP! You get an IEP! Everybody gets an IEP!" Kids are all different. Why should they be educated all the same way?

When my geography lover wanted to spend hours using Google Earth to zoom in on Alaska and find out what the population was for each city or tiny town, he had that freedom. When my bird lover wanted to spend the day viewing birds in the coastal areas of Massachusetts, we went. We rearranged the living room so our budding composer can more easily access the piano, which he plays several times a day.

I've seen incredible growth in all my children, and being there to support them has brought me so many joys: unexpected hugs from my youngest, lessons on computer security from my oldest, and, from the middle child, free consulting on birdsong identification. These are beautiful flowers that I can enjoy.

Side benefits of homeschooling include flexible bedtimes and mealtimes! We can all eat with Dad who sometimes doesn't get home from the office until late. And there is flexibility during field trips! Do you want to linger on the nature trail while you strain to hear a particular bird? Sure. Do you want to stop in the middle of the aquarium to tell me new details from the day when you were at the beach and a jellyfish stung you? Go ahead. We have all day.

And because we had all day, every day, when it came time for my oldest two to graduate and leave the house for an out-of-state college experience, I was ready. (I believed they were, too!) I had had my time with them.

HOMESCHOOLING CHALLENGES

There were and continue to be many challenges! I think of my active middle child. He had a hard time sitting still while I read aloud, so I allowed him to throw and catch a football while he listened. Another time, my oldest, as a fourth-grader, wanted to read the book *Freakonomics*. Some of the content was a little mature for a nine-year-old so we read it together.

As a homeschool mom, I have to be able to analyze and solve problems when things don't go according to plan. How do you teach English when the baby needs so much attention? Squeeze it in during naptime. How do you make sure the children are getting enough physical activity, especially during the winter? We tried a bunch of things: Wii Fit, snow shoveling, even football in the backyard! During the high school years, being able to participate in winter sports at the local public school gave them plenty of ways to stay in shape during our cold and dark New England winters.

When they would balk at an assignment, I would try to find out what the issue was. Often it was as simple as asking: Is it too easy or too hard? I would try to find that sweet spot where an assignment was enough of a challenge to make it worth the effort, but not so much that they would be discouraged and give up.

My middle son, when he was a pre-teen, had a tendency to see things that were wrong and voice his concerns—to the exclusion of anything else. Just like on my developing plant, this was a runner that needed to go in another direction! One day, I told him gently but forthrightly that constantly thinking negative thoughts wasn't productive. "It's not a good way to live," I said. It was a quick conversation and with some kids, "lectures" such as this one wouldn't be fruitful. But I knew my son, and the reasoned approach worked immediately. He still picked up on what was wrong with the world, but his optimistic side came out more often.

Occasionally, what *I* thought was a great idea was not always well-received. This year, I bought a specialized curriculum for teaching geography. By the end of the year, students would be able to produce a map of the world freehand from memory! Despite my enthusiasm, my youngest just didn't take to it. He did try to please me, but he also complained a good bit. He struggled with sketching what he felt were less than perfect maps. Instead of pressing on, I humbly admitted it wasn't working. What kind of geography project could he do that would prove his knowledge but draw on his love of music? I suggested he memorize "Yakko's World," a song that lists just about every country in the world to the tune of the Mexican Hat Dance. In the animated version, as Yakko sings, he points to each country. Now my son is excited to practice, and daily recites as much as he can.

Sometimes the challenges come from the outside. My oldest wanted to join the soccer team at the local public high school. Unfortunately, he wound up having to sit out the season while the administration jumped through bureaucratic hoops to update one paragraph in their policy in order to allow him to play. Now the updated policy has turned out to benefit other homeschooled students in our town—including his younger brother—who wanted to participate in sports at the high school.

Last year, my local superintendent's office sent me a letter saying I hadn't filed the "Letter of Intent" required to homeschool in my state.

Because I keep good records, I was able to prove to them that I had. (Pro tip: Always send a letter of intent via certified mail!) I personally showed them the postcard with the signature of the person who received my letter. It turned out there had been a change in personnel and that was why some homeschool records couldn't be located.

Though such challenges have been considerable, the rewards have been greater. In his senior year, my oldest won a Gold Key Scholastic writing award for his essay arguing why we should get rid of the penny. I remember attending the award ceremony for the regional winners in Boston. The mom sitting next to me told me which school her daughter, who was also getting an award, attended. Later, I discovered it was a high-priced private high school. It made me feel good. And, truthfully, there are some very good private schools. We would have been able to afford it if I had gone back to work. But then it would have been someone else hearing formative memories of a jellyfish sting. Or perhaps no one. And would there have been time for deep-dives into Google Earth or debate research? Would teachers at school see how and when to give a gentle nudge in the right direction? To me, the value of a homeschool educational environment is priceless.

And it may be that the greater rewards have not come from the academic setting. As seniors, each of my two older boys was honored with their public high school's varsity athletic team's "Unsung Hero" award. To have educational entities external to our "HI Road Academy" recognize the boys' humility and integrity were wonderfully gratifying moments. "Well done, good and faithful servant[s]" (Matthew 25:21, The New King James Version).

PARTING WORDS

My two homeschool graduates are doing well. One just graduated from college with an engineering degree. The other, also pursuing engineering, is halfway through his program. They both are following the Lord and are seeking to do His will. What more could we ask for?

"Train up a child in the way he should go: and when he is old, he will not depart from it." Guide your children to climb toward the Light while they are young, and they will bloom for the world to see.

24

BOB CRAGHEAD

Bob is a long-haired, big-bearded, daily kilt-wearing, Viking-looking, stay-at-home dad who sometimes moonlights as an online college professor teaching various courses. He is a self-proclaimed Facebook enlightener who likes to stir pots and poke social sacred cows when he is not posting braggadocio photos of his family's adventurous escapades. He holds a bachelor's from Brigham Young University in English and a master's from the University of Utah in Education, Culture, and Society. He and his wife Molli (who works in human resources) are the proud and extremely humble parents of two daughters and a son, ages eight to thirteen. When not adventuring with his family, he likes to go to the gym where he often, at present, finds some of his only real adult social interactions.

ABOUT OUR FAMILY

I was sitting at the kitchen table Easter Sunday morning, 2020. The kids woke up early and arranged their homemade Easter cards at the places my wife and I usually sit. Holidays are celebrations in our house, especially the minor ones. Since the kids were babies, we have had green pancakes and treasure hunts for Saint Patrick's Day, heart-shaped pancakes and pink milk for Valentine's Day, and on our individual birthdays, the rest of the family makes us the breakfast of our choice. And then later we choose which restaurant we go to for dinner. Sometimes I wonder if maybe we shouldn't have instituted these traditions. They are a lot of work, and the kids expect them and look forward to them year after year.

But it's all worth it because the kids have organically established traditions of their own. For each holiday, one of the things they do is make my wife and me individual themed holiday cards, and they often spend much of the prior week covertly constructing them. This particular Easter seemed like all others with cards of bunnies, "I love you," and "Happy Easter Dad!"

Later in the day, my oldest (thirteen) let it slip that my card took forever to make. I quickly located it—really looked at it for the first time—and my jaw dropped. This was not just the drawing of a rabbit as I had previously supposed. The bunny's fur had texture, and it was arranged in a way that it flowed and curved, making circular motions around the haunches and feet, simulating real fur. "What is this?" I asked. "Thread," she said. "Sewing thread. And it took me forever to glue the individual threads to get it right." The threads were one single layer perfectly and succinctly aligned on the paper. It was a marvel in artistry. I looked up at her in wonder as she beamed. She has always been artistic, but this had gone to an entirely different level. Such focus, such dedication, such patience, such engineering, all at thirteen years old.

In addition to being an artist, she has read more books than I can count, some multiple times. She has also fabricated her own dollhouses, swords for her brother, a paper doll version of me wearing one of my kilts with a multicolored tartan (complete with flowing long hair made of curled yarn), and much more.

Her sister who is ten, and a completely different personality from her older sister, is our extreme sport adrenaline junkie. She loves rock climbing, skiing, death-defying heights, the wind in her hair, and going as fast as she can whether on the ski slopes, on her mountain bike, or on her skateboard.

She also is a master navigator, finding the quickest routes in one of the obsessions she shares with me: geocaching. She also is becoming a very accomplished baker, always begging to make cookies and brownies and other treats. And she is usually the first to ask me if she can help with whatever meal I may be preparing.

Our son, at present, is an extremely strong-willed and kindhearted eight-year-old. He is a rambunctious ninja who loves all sorts of gadgets and can identify practically any animal alive and extrapolate details of each, including sleep habits, diets, temperaments—you name it. He loves to be outside and has an unwavering passion for collecting sticks. Sticks of all sizes and varieties, which he says remind him of various things including swords, staffs, animals—basically things that aid in his vivid imaginary play. Like his oldest sister he likes to fabricate things, and he has made bird feeders, cardboard box cars, swords, and daggers. He creates his own board games, complete with intricate rules and game pieces. He is also the best at sharing anything and everything, whether it is his favorite chocolate donut from 7-Eleven or his most prized gadgets and toys.

I attribute much of their individuality, talents, and personalities—all the things that make our children each uniquely them—to the choice we made to homeschool. Of course, everyone's story is unique, and I am certainly not implying that parents who do not homeschool do not have fully developed children. But for us, the choice to homeschool our children has given them the environments, opportunities, and freedom to explore and develop their natural talents and attributes.

WHAT I LOVE ABOUT HOMESCHOOLING

Homeschooling really never entered our minds as something we would do with our children, until it did. And when it did, it entered with fury, made sense, and felt right. I have spent my entire education career as a college instructor trying to deprogram my students. Trying to get into their socially constructed heads that learning should be, above all else, fun. Learning is an exhilarating, innate, glorious wonder. We are born with the desire to continually learn new things, to improve, to grow, to thrive. Simply watch babies and very young children learning a new task and this is readily evident. However, like most people, my students have been programmed through society and personal observations that learning is an onerous and grueling process that one must endure in order to access the good life. Most folks see learning and education much the same way as they see taking medicine—the stuff tastes awful, and the experience is excruciating, but if you force yourself to gag it down, it will make you better.

Around the time we were getting ready to enroll our oldest in kindergarten, a few of my friends, very educated and brilliant friends who I love and trust, had started homeschooling their kids. I had also recently read Peter Gray's powerful book *Free to Learn* and devoured every page. Homeschooling and the freedom it would give us to nurture our children in the learning environments and philosophies I have tried to instill in my students just seemed like it was meant to be. And so we began.

Our approach is more of an unschooling one where we simply live life and learn as we do. We wanted to create an environment for the kids where natural and organic learning flourishes, where they feel free to learn with no pressures, deadlines, tests, grades, and the like. In fact, what we really want is for them to live life and progress and learn without realizing that they are "learning" at all. Having the kids home allows us to go on adventure after adventure. We are avid bicyclists, hikers, geocachers, and explorers. We have hiked to multiple Anasazi ruins in the Four Corners area of the U.S., hiked slot canyons with amazing waterfalls, explored Arches and Bryce Canyon National Parks, and stayed in old ranger cabins throughout Utah—we continually have adventures.

One of the most rewarding things about homeschooling is that it simply gives us that chance to be together as a family, with greater flexibility do go wherever and whenever we want. And the kids experience learning organically, in their own way and at their own pace. We often have had deep conversations in the car about civil rights, social justice, racism, education, history, religion, the need to question assumptions, and other subjects that come up naturally. It truly has been a grand adventure, one that we are so glad we embarked on, and one we continue.

HOMESCHOOLING CHALLENGES

Of course, homeschooling does present its challenges. My kids will tell you the thing they hate most about being homeschooled is when folks ask them what grade they are in, and then try to guess based on their ages. Although homeschooling is prevalent enough now that those same people usually get the picture when my kids roll their eyes at me. "Oh, are you homeschooled?"

For me the most challenging part is mostly an inner turmoil, asking myself questions such as, "Did we make the right decision to keep them out of school and educate them ourselves? Have we messed them up for the rest of their lives? Will they be able to get into college? How will they do when they do get into college?"

When my self-inflicted anxieties arise or negative thoughts occur, I look at my kids and I see how they can figure things out and solve problems. How they can research and learn about the things that interest them. How they can think thoroughly about societal issues and see various viewpoints. I see how socially adroit they are and how people often comment about this. And so we keep going—from one adventure to the next—continually learning, continually growing, continually exploring, and continually enjoying the ride.

PARTING WORDS

The advice I give to those considering homeschooling is simply to believe in yourselves and make it your own. Do not get caught up in what everyone else is doing, and certainly don't continually compare your kids to other kids and what they are learning in public schools (even if it helps you justify homeschooling). In fact, not comparing ourselves to others, period, is a wise practice. Teach your kids how to learn. Teach them how to research. Instill in them a strong sense of self-efficacy, which means that they can figure things out and make things happen. Teach them to be problem solvers and give them opportunities to practice this. Teach them that it is okay not to know everything. What's more important is that they learn how to find answers for themselves and continually discover new things. Teach them how to evaluate information. But more than anything else, have fun and enjoy the process. If you are not having fun, then you are probably not doing it correctly.

And finally, one bit of advice and wisdom that a mentor once taught me, that I now call "The why and the how principle." So often in life we don't begin something we really want to do because we don't know how to do it. But the "how" is not the most important thing you need to have. The most important thing is the "why." Why do you want to do something? If you have a strong vision of the "why," you will invent the "how," and you will often invent it as you go. So, if you are thinking about homeschooling, ask yourself why. Why do you want to homeschool? If you can get a clear vision of that, then begin the grand adventure of inventing and figuring out the how. And if your experience is anything like ours, it will be glorious.

AFTERWORD

by Kathy Oaks

This year, 2020, is an interesting one to be living through. When Brynn asked me to co-edit this book with her, we were already two months into the COVID-19 pandemic's stay-at-home restrictions where I live. I wrote my essay for the book (see chapter 2) before reading any of the other essays, and I wasn't sure what to expect. On the one hand, the essays are meant to be an encouragement to homeschoolers, transcending beyond our current circumstances. On the other hand, the authors had just lived through some trying times that limited homeschoolers' ability to get out and see the world, which is one of the things we prize. Would that frustration come through in their essays?

As I worked my way through the essays, I didn't see that frustration. Instead, I was struck by the positivity of the common themes that ran through all of them. Even though these families live in different places, come from different circumstances, and have different (sometimes very different) approaches on how to best educate their children, they all are deeply grateful for the opportunity to homeschool their children. It didn't just fall into their laps, it required work to make it happen. And, after finishing this book, I definitely felt that it is worth the effort for all these families.

That's not the only similarity, though. Even when they didn't specifically use these words (and many did), the authors all felt strongly that the ability to tailor their children's education to each individual was one of the things they appreciate most about homeschooling. Flexibility is another. Flexibility allows for tailoring the education, but it's more than that. It's a mindset that homeschooling fosters, that of a willingness to try something different. It helps the whole family fit homeschooling into their lives, because everyone can make it their own. As you've seen, homeschooling can happen first thing in the morning or after work hours. It can be summer camps or online classes. It can be working on a farm or taking field trips or traveling your country or the world.

Halfway through the editing process, circumstances changed again. George Floyd was murdered by a police officer in Minneapolis, Minnesota, and protests against police brutality and racism swept across the world. Several of the authors were personally affected by the protests, in a variety of ways. The more so for our minority writers, who have felt the impact of discriminatory practices their whole lives. Some of the authors, along with their families, protested, volunteered to clean and donated supplies or money in the aftermath of unrest, and even left their homes temporarily to keep their families safe. And yet, they kept writing positive, helpful essays on the joys of homeschooling, even when their neighborhoods and their lives had been negatively impacted.

From these essays, it's easy to see that there are so many things that bring us together, even though homeschoolers are a very diverse bunch. Not everyone is aware of this great diversity of homeschoolers, even within the various homeschool communities. And plenty of people between homeschool communities have differences of opinion, both along educational philosophy lines and along religious lines. Now is a great time to open the discussion and show the world what homeschooling has to offer. Brynn and I have worked to make sure a whole spectrum of voices is heard. And yet one book isn't enough.

It's not enough to just be inclusive, to include a diversity of voices. As you've seen in the essays, it's a lot harder for some families to homeschool than others. And there are families who aren't represented here at all because they just don't have access to enough resources to homeschool. We have a great opportunity in these times of change to bring people together as parents who all want the best for our children, no matter our backgrounds. We must work together to make the world a place where all parents can be free to choose the best way to educate their children, free from prejudice, free from fear, free from poverty, free from barriers to achieving their full potential, and free to celebrate who they are—culturally, spiritually, physically. If any one of us isn't free, none of us is truly free. I hope this book is one small step in the right direction.

Recommended Resources

Books and Articles by Our Contributors

"The Art of Knowing When to Push," *Home School Life Magazine*, by Carrie Pomeroy

"Cooking with What's in the Bag: Unschooling as the CSA Model of Learning," *Life Learning Magazine*, by Carrie Pomeroy

Five Minute Devotions for the Homeschool Mom, by Tina Nahid

Flourish: Balance for Homeschool Moms, by Mary Jo Tate

Help Me Homeschool!, by Faye Badenhop

Homeschool Adventures: Learning Through the Power of Field Trips, by Melissa Calapp

Homeschoolers Are Not Hermits, by Kathy Oaks

The Homeschoolers Are Not Hermits Quick Start Guide, by Kathy Oaks

Homeschooling and Working while Shaping Amazing Learners, by LM Preston

Just for Today's Homeschooling Mom, by Michelle Huddleston

Moments of Grace: Daily Reflections for the Homeschool Mom, by Tina Nahid

"Relief is Everything: The Homeschooling Journey of a Special Needs Family," *SEA Homeschoolers*, by Regina Merchant

Road Schooling, by Kathy Oaks

The Seven Year Ditch, by Alyson Long

"Unit Study Idea: The African-American Struggle for Civil Rights, Past and Present," *Home School Life Magazine*, by Carrie Pomeroy

Blogs and Websites by Our Contributors

Barndt.org/blog: Ann Barndt

EclecticBibliophile.com: Mary Jo Tate

EmpoweredSteps.com: LM Preston

Facebook.com/groups/outtaboxhomeschooling: Michelle Huddleston

FlourishAtHome.com: Mary Jo Tate

HEART Community Facebook group: Crissi Allen

HomeschoolandWork.blogspot.com: LM Preston

HomeschoolGroupHug.com: Alyson Long

HomeschoolersNotHermits.com: Kathy Oaks

Homeschooling2e.com: Mary Paul

Squibix.net: Dan Archibald
WildToes.com: Kelley Christie (Boston area)
WithTheHuddlestons.com/blog: Michelle Huddleston
WorldTravelFamily.com: Alyson Long

Books

The 5 Habits of Highly Successful Homeschoolers, by Rachel and Oliver DeMille
The Three R's: Grades K-3, by Ruth Beechick
Better Late Than Early, by Raymond and Dorothy Moore
The Brave Learner, by Julie Bogart
Creative Schools, by Ken Robinson
Dumbing Us Down, by John Taylor Gatto
Educating the Wholehearted Child, by Clay and Sally Clarkson
For the Children's Sake, by Susan Schaeffer Macaulay
Free to Learn, by Peter Gray
Guerrilla Learning, by Grace Llewellyn and Amy Silver
Hacking Your Education, by Dale Stephens
Home is Where the Learning Is, by Valerie J. Steimle
Home is Where the Learning Is For High School, by Valerie J. Steimle
Home Grown, by Ben Hewitt
Home Learning Year By Year, by Rebecca Rupp
Honey for a Child's Heart: The Imaginative Use of Books in Family Life, by Gladys Hunt
How Children Fail, by John Holt
How Children Learn, by John Holt
How to Grow a Young Reader: A Parent's Guide to Books for Kids, by Kathryn Lindskoog and Ranelda Mack Hunsicker
I Learn Better By Teaching Myself, by Agnes Leistico
I Saw the Angel in the Marble, by Chris and Ellyn Davis
Growing Without Schooling, by John Holt
Learning All the Time, by John Holt
Passion-Driven Education, by Connor Boyack
The Read-Aloud Family, by Sarah Mackenzie
School Education: Developing a Curriculum, by Charlotte Mason
Senior High: A Home-Designed Form+U+La by Barbara Edtl Shelton
Skip College: Launch Your Career Without Debt, Distractions, or a Degree, Connor Boyack
Teach Your Own, by John Holt and Patrick Farenga

Teaching from Rest, by Sarah Mackenzie

Teaching The Trivium, by Harvey and Laurie Bluedorn

A Thomas Jefferson Education, by Oliver DeMille

A Thomas Jefferson Education Home Companion, by Oliver DeMille, Rachel DeMille, and Diann Jeppson

The Unhurried Homeschooler, Durenda Wilson

Unschooled, by Kerry McDonald

Unschooling Rules, by Clark Aldrich

Weapons of Mass Instruction, by John Taylor Gatto

Workshops Work!, by Patricia Zaballos

The Well-Trained Mind, by Jessie Wise and Susan Wise Bauer

You Can Teach Your Child Successfully: Grades 4-8, by Ruth Beechick

Resources for Parents

CambridgeInternational.org: IGCSE International General Certificate of Secondary Education

CathyDuffyReviews.com: Comprehensive reviews of homeschool materials

ChristianUnschooling.com: Christian Unschooling

ClassicalConversations.com: Classical Christian Community

Education.PenelopeTrunk.com: Blog about homeschooling, unschooling, Asperger's, and dyslexia

FreeRangeKids.com: Free Range Kids

FulltimeFamilies.com: RVing Family Community

HappyHomeschooling.com: Happy Homeschooling

HomeschoolAustralia.com: The Educating Parent: Homeschooling and Unschooling in Australia

JohnHoltGWS.com: John Holt: Growing Without Schooling

JoyfullyRejoycing.com: Radical Unschooling

RainbowResource.com: Learning Tools for Homes and Schools

HSLDA.org/Get-Started: Homeschool Legal Defense Association: Exploring Homeschooling

IDENetwork.org: International Democratic Education Network

NaturalChild.org: Natural Child Project

NBTSC.org: Not-Back-to-School Camp

OaxacaBorn.com: Rhythms of Classical Gifted Homeschooling

PatriciaZaballos.com/blog: Wonder Farm: Fostering a Love of Learning for Homeschooling Families

ProjectWorldschool.com: Project Worldschool retreats and conferences

PsychologyToday.com/us/blog/Freedom-Learn: Peter Gray's Freedom to Learn blog

PurvaBrown.com: The Classical Unschooler

ReadAloudrevival.com: Podcast and book lists to foster a read-aloud family culture

SEA Homeschoolers.com: Secular, Eclectic, Academic Homeschoolers

SecularEclecticAcademic.com: Secular homeschooling books

SecularHomeschooler.com: Secular Homeschooler resources and lists

Self-Directed.org: The Alliance for Self-Directed Education

UnCollege.org: Unschooling college, and gap year travel

WellEducatedHeart.com: Well-Educated Heart/Libraries of Hope

Resources for Children

ABCya.com: Educational games (PreK-6)

ArtForKidsHub.com: Free instructional art videos (Pre-teen)

CNN.com/CNN10 Daily: 10-minute news coverage for students (older kids)

Coursera.org: Online courses (older kids)

TheCrashCourse.com: Free AP level video courses

Dreambox.com/homeschool: Dreambox Learning online lessons and games (K-8)

Ed.Ted.com: TedEd website with videos and teaching resources

Education.com: Educational games, worksheets, and activities (PreK-5)

ExtraCredits.site: Computer programming and history videos

GoNoodle.com: Movement and mindfulness videos

Khan Academy Online learning platform

TheKidShouldSeeThis.com: Smart Videos for Curious Minds of All Ages

Masterclass.com: Online classes (older kids)

ProdigyGame.com: Math game (K-8, online or via an app)

RosettaStone.com: Online foreign language learning

SmarterEveryDay.com: Science technology, and engineering videos

STMath.com: PreK-8 math instruction

Time4Learning.com: Flexible online curriculum

Udemy.com: Online classes (older kids)

WhatsInside.it/videos: Science, technology, and engineering videos

Youtube.com/MarkRober: New ideas, science, and engineering

About the Authors

Brynn Steimle, along with her husband, has home educated their three children (by birth and adoption) since 2014. She is a children's book author, former organizer of the Hong Kong Homeschool Meetup Group, and has taught university Family Science classes. She is a member of The Church of Jesus Christ of Latter-day Saints and has a master's degree in Marriage, Family, and Human Development from Brigham Young University. She currently resides in New England in the USA.

Kathy Oaks is a photographer, author, and educator who is passionate about travel and learning. She lives in the Midwest region of the U.S. with her husband and three sons. Kathy is dedicated to helping parents and kids who want to take a non-traditional approach to education. She has written three additional books on homeschooling: *Homeschoolers Are Not Hermits*, to support families as they make the transition from conventional schooling to the adventure of homeschooling, *The Homeschoolers Are Not Hermits Quick Start Guide*, and *Road Schooling*, to bring her family's joy of travel to others.

Author bios for all contributors are available at
www.brynnsteimle.com/whyilovehomeschoolingbook

Made in the USA
Middletown, DE
01 August 2020